AF505759
ville (C)
38
(C)
Regis (C)
5
ain (A)
39
Priest Lake
Kootenay R.
Immaculate Heart of Mary (C) 1845
St. Ignatius (C) 1845
Pend Oreille Lake
Pend Oreille R.
The Assumption (C) 1845
Flathead Lake
Swan R.
St. Francis Borgia (C) 1845
Colville R.
St. Michael's (C) 1844
1842
1846
Spokane R.
Sacred Heart (C)
Coeur d'Alene R.
Coeur d'Alene 1843
St. Joe R.
Coeur d'Alene Lake
Bitterroot River
St. Mary's (C) 1841
Lapwai (A) 1836
Clearwater River
Snake River
Snake R.
Kamiah (A) 1839
ort Walla Walla (C)
838
Waiilatpu (A) 1836
a R.
Walla Walla R.
St. Ann's (C) 1847
PRINCIPAL MISSIONS AND STATIONS
Lower Columbia River and Its Tributaries
1834 — 1847
LEGEND: (A)—American Board
(C)—Catholic
(M)—Methodist

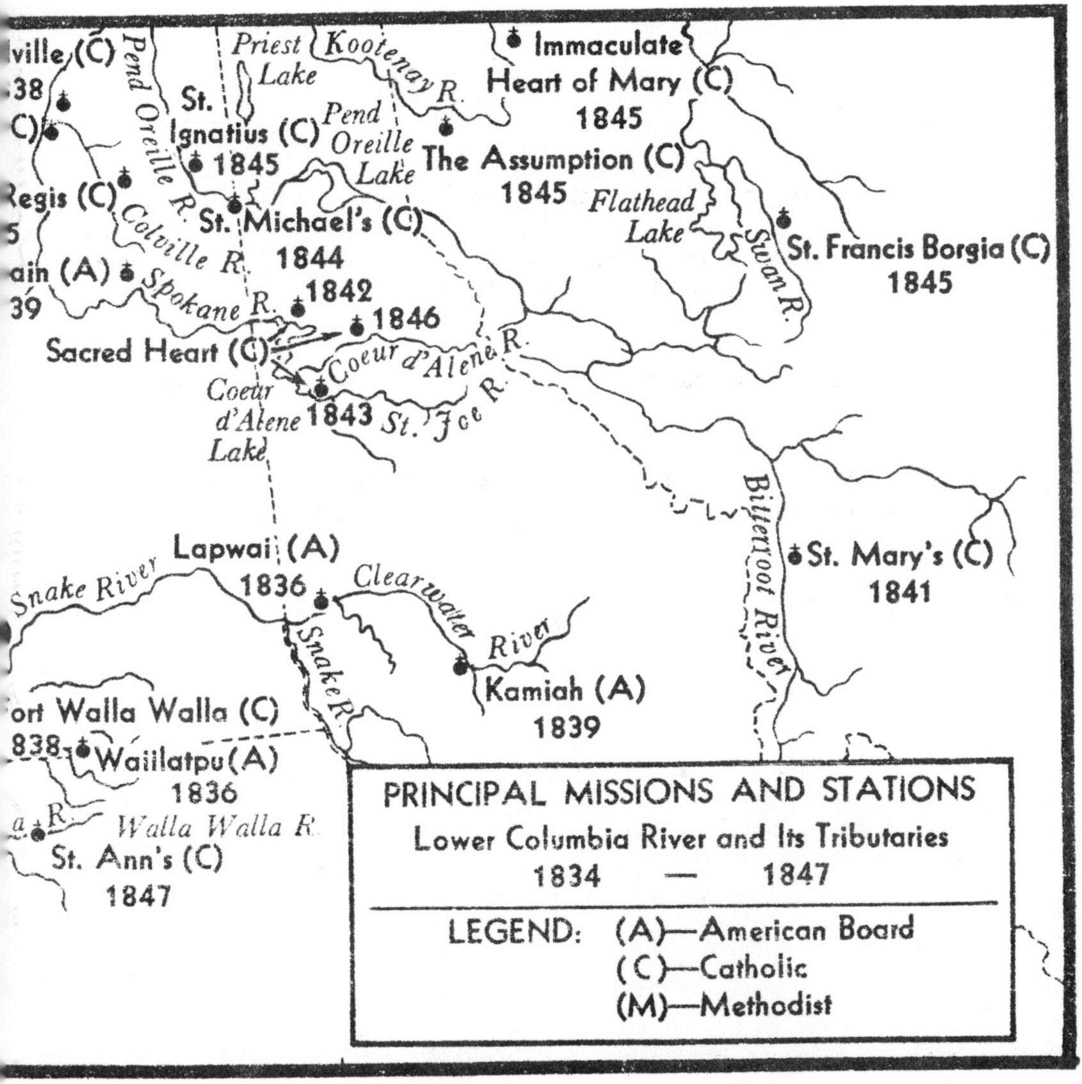

Library of Congress Cataloging in Publication Data

Mudge, Zachariah Atwell, 1813-1888.
    Sketches of mission life among the Indians of Oregon.

    Includes index.
    1.Indians   of   North   America—Oregon—Missions.   2.Missions—
Oregon. I. title.

E78.06M86              1983            979.5′00497            83-14594
ISBN 0-87770-308-6


Endsheet maps courtesy of National Park Service.

# SKETCHES OF MISSION LIFE
## AMONG THE INDIANS OF OREGON

# SKETCHES

# MISSION LIFE

AMONG THE

## INDIANS OF OREGON.

———

**New-York:**

PUBLISHED BY CARLTON & PORTER,

SUNDAY-SCHOOL UNION, 200 MULBERRY-STREET.

The Zachariah Mudge *Sketches of Mission Life Among the Indians of Oregon* is not listed in Howes but Howes does list his *The Missionary Teacher, a Memoir of Cyrus Shepard ...* New York, 1848, 221 p. 16mo. Shepard was a very early immigrant to Oregon as he crossed the plains with Nathaniel J. Wyeth in 1834.

The Zachariah Mudge *Sketches ...* is a rare book but copies are held by several Pacific Northwest libraries, namely: University of Montana, Washington State University and Willamette University (Salem, OR).

The Mudge *Sketches ...* is listed in Smith as M-7132.

# SKETCHES

## OF

## MISSION LIFE

### AMONG THE

## INDIANS OF OREGON

ZACHARIAH ATWELL MUDGE

YE GALLEON PRESS

**FAIRFIELD, WASHINGTON**

FORT WALLA WALLA IN 1857.  FROM A PEN SKETCH OF THAT DATE

Zachariah Atwell Mudge, author of this rare Pacific Northwest book, SKETCHES OF MISSION LIFE AMONG THE INDIANS OF OREGON, was a member of a well-known New England family going back to 1649 or earlier. Zachariah Mudge was born in Orrington, Penobscot County, Maine, son of James Mudge, on July 2, 1813. He was educated at the Lynn, Massachusetts Academy and Wesleyan University, which institution he left before graduating. After teaching in Massachusetts and in Mississippi he entered the ministry of the Methodist Episcopal Church in 1840 and was stationed at various places in Massachusetts. In 1854 he was given an honorary A.M. degree from Wesleyan University. From 1859 to 1862 he was editor of *The Guide to Holiness*. During his pastoral career of 45 years he found time to prepare for publication a large number of works of fiction for Sunday School libraries. He was also the author of a number of non-fiction works. Besides the *Sketches of Mission Life Among the Indians of Oregon*, New York, 1854; he wrote *The Christian Statesman, A Portraiture of Sir Thomas Buxton* (1865); *Witch Hill, A History of Salem Witchcraft* (1870); *Arctic Heroes* (1874); *North Pole Voyages* (1875); *History of Suffolk County, Massachusetts* (1879); *Fur-Clad Adventurers* (1880); and others of similar character. It is believed that he never lived in or traveled to the Pacific Northwest. Death came in 1888.

This information was furnished by Nancy Pryor, Washington Room, Washington State Library, Olympia.

# TABLE OF CONTENTS

# LIST OF ILLUSTRATIONS

# PREFACE

The materials from which these sketches have been drawn were given to the writer by a returned lay missionary, who had been nearly nine years in Oregon, under the directions of the Methodist Episcopal Missionary Board. The author having heard the substance of many of them narrated, in social conversation, was impressed with the belief that they ought not to be lost. He, therefore, induced the missionary to make a summary statement of the facts, the only presentation of them which his pressing secular duties allowed; and these facts the writer has written out in the familiar style of these "sketches."

His desire is, that they may stimulate the sympathy of the reader for Christian missionaries, and their work; and thus prove a drop in the swelling tide of gospel influences, which are bearing the Church onward to the rescue of a lost world.

**Canoe Voyage on the Columbia**

# MISSION LIFE IN OREGON

### THE VOYAGE TO OREGON

NLY THOSE WHO EXPERIENCE THEM CAN KNOW the feelings of persons who go to preach the gospel in a heathen land. They leave well-tried friends to associate with those who may, perhaps, hate them for their Master's sake. They go to perform untried duties, to endure afflictions yet unknown, and to submit to privations which must make the remembrance of lost blessings both pleasant and sad. In the hour when they bid adieu to home, they need the abounding grace of God in their own hearts, and the warm sympathy and the fervent prayers of the people of God. It is not gold which they go to seek, but souls, for whom Christ died; not worldly honor, but an immortal crown.

In the spring of 1839, the Rev. Jason Lee returned from Oregon, where he had been laboring as a missionary about five years, and brought with him five Flat Head Indians. The object of his visit was to arouse the Church to a deeper interest in the red men of that far-off territory, that he might be able to return with more missionaries for the great work. Missionary meetings were held in various places, and great interest in the subject was manifested by the Churches generally. A large reinforcement of the devoted band of missionaries already in Oregon was procured, who met in New-York, in September of that year, where enthusiastic meetings were held, in anticipation of their departure.

In October they bade adieu to their native land and Christian friends, and, in company with several brethren of the American Board, who were going as missionaries to the Sandwich Islands, embarked in a fine ship for a long and perilous voyage. We cannot detail the particulars of their feelings and experience during an *eight* months' passage. Most of the time they were shut up in their floating home on the ocean. Dayly they gazed upon the wide, wide waters; thought of the friends who were far away praying for them, and the wild sons of the forest, for whose rescue from moral death they longed to be toiling. They thought, too, of that God whose dwelling-place is everywhere — in heaven, on the dry land, and on the ocean; whose eyes never slumbers, and whose arm is never withdrawn from those who do his will. They felt a sweet peace while they thought and often sung, —

"This awful God is ours,
Our Father and our Love;
He will send down his heavenly powers,
To carry us above."

Every Sabbath, when the weather permitted, they had preaching twice; and every morning and evening, prayer meetings. Bible classes were also formed, so that the time passed away as pleasantly as the nature of the circumstances would permit; for the reader will not be surprised to learn that *sea-sickness*, that troublesome attendant upon the inexperienced voyager, disturbed the comfort of most of the company. They landed at Rio Janeiro and Valparaiso, and obtained fresh provisions, including the delicious fruit of those countries, which was especially acceptable after they had been denied so long the sight of such food.

They landed on the Sandwich Islands in April, and were received with Christian courtesy by the missionaries laboring there.

As they approached the Columbia River, every eye gazed intensely in the direction of the foaming waters upon the dangerous rocks at its mouth. Soon the mist lifted up, and the long-wished-for land was hailed, with sincere gratitude to Him who had kindly saved them from all the dangers of the seas. They landed at Fort Vancouver, June 1, 1840. The hearts of the brethren already there, who had been so long toiling with but few Christian associates, were made glad at their arrival. Their gladness was mingled with grief, however, while they conveyed to their friends the tidings that one of their number, brother Cyrus Shephard, had been laid in the grave, after a painful and protracted sickness. This brother's memoirs have been published by the Methodist Sunday School Union.* His name is the treasure of the Church.

The company tarried at the Fort eleven days, during which time one of the newly-arrived company was married to the Rev. Daniel Lee, who had been six years already engaged in this field of labor. Here arrangements were made to distribute the company into several bands, to be sent to different fields of labor. Some left for Puget Sound; others were appointed to the Willamette Valley; and still others for the Calapoosa country, far up the Willamette. Those whose history we shall more particularly follow were appointed to the Dalles station, in Middle Oregon, between the President's Range and the Rocky Mountains. A pioneer company had been laboring there for some time, with considerable success. It was an important location, not only for the influence it was expected the mission would exert upon the Indian tribes, but because it lay in the line of travel from the States to the fruitful valley of the Willamette; and it was hoped, therefore, that the

* Youth's Library, No. 412.

emigrants might also be met, on entering the country, with the sound of the gospel.

We shall have occasion, in the course of these sketches, to describe the voyage up the Columbia which our friends were now to make; we will, therefore, leave them toiling to complete their long journey, and to find a rude but comfortable resting place in their new home.

## THE HOME OF THE MISSIONARIES

At the Dalles of the Columbia River the missionaries whose history we are about to sketch found a rude but comfortable home. The missionary already there, anticipating their arrival in the country, had started down the Columbia to assist them in their journey, and fortunately met them just above Fort Vancouver. This mission station was established in 1838 by the Rev. D. Lee and the Rev. H.K.W. Perkins. It was on the south bank of the Columbia, two hundred miles from its mouth, and one hundred miles from Fort Vancouver, the nearest place of communication with the white inhabitants of the territory. The missionaries of the Willamette Valley were one hundred and fifty miles off, and Dr. Whitman, of the American Board, one hundred and thirty-five miles.

The house which our friends occupied was erected at the commencement of the mission, and was, of course, a rough abode, and built, even in its rough style, with much labor and inconvenience. The logs were brought by hand, with the aid of the Indians, about eighty rods. The boards for the floor and ceiling were sawed out by hand. The shingles were made twelve miles from the spot, and brought on pack-horses. At first it consisted of one room, but now a kitchen and wood-house had been added. Its precise site was upon the *upper*, south bank of the Columbia, about half a mile from its channel. The *front* door of the house opened toward the river, in which direction was a fine yard, inclosed by a high wall of earth, affording a pleasant play-ground for the children. From the south end of the house the door opened into a square of nearly an acre of ground, making a kind of "common" or public promenade. Upon the opposite side of the square, on the south, stood the church, a plain log building; and near it a schoolhouse, which, if not beautiful to the eye as many which ornament the growing villages of the States, was, to the eye of the *Christian*, very beautiful. On the east was the house of Mr. Perkins, who had assisted, as we have stated, to commence the mission; and opposite his residence, on the west, was what the missionaries pleasantly called their "civilized barn," because it was in the style of those in the settled parts of the country. Near this was a workshop, which completed the settlement of the whites. A short distance from the square was a beautiful spring of pure water, which the Indians called "Wasco;" hence the name "Wasco-pam," which sometimes gave title to the mission. This spring irrigated a garden plot, from which, in their season, the mission families obtained their vegetables. The vicinity of this station was not thickly wooded, pine and oak growing here and there. A little further west the forest became dense, and toward the east trees disappeared altogether, and a succession of barren hills rose in the distance.

From this beautiful location the Columbia could be seen, three miles above and six below; the lofty summits of Mount Adams and of Mount Hood were in full view, on the north; and, by going a mile to a more elevated position, nine snow-covered summits of the President's Range could be seen.

In this spot, made beautiful by nature, but around which savage man had his "habitations of cruelty," because sitting in moral night, our missionary friends began their labor. They had not chosen this far-off home in the wilderness to amass wealth, nor to gratify a spirit of adventure. They had left dear friends and valued Christian privileges, and willingly made the untaught Indians their neighbors, that they might teach them a Saviour's love. It must not be thought that they never *felt* their loneliness, — that they never *thought* of the loved ones under the paternal roof. The society of the red man is at all times cheerless, because of his degradation; and sometimes *alarming*, as will be seen in the course of these sketches. But when God, as he graciously did, owned their labors, and the wilderness was, *in any measure*, made to "bud and blossom," then did they rejoice that they were counted worthy to suffer such things for Christ's sake.

----•----

### CLIMATE AND SOIL

The climate of Oregon is much milder than that in the states of the same latitude. In the Willamette Valley the warm season is very dry; there is no rain sometimes for a period of six months. The winters are very rainy. The climate, one hundred and fifty miles further from the ocean, is different. The vicinity of mountainous regions, where the snow never wholly disappears, has an influence in making the evenings cool and the air always clear and agreeable. For six months the sky is seldom mantled with a cloud: the heavens seem continually to smile, and the earth to be glad. The winters are colder then on the sea-coast, and for two months there is some snow. The spring rains suffice for the winter wheat, which will come to maturity without further watering; but corn, potatoes, and most garden vegetables require irrigation.

The soil in the Willamette Valley is excellent, especially for wheat. A farmer of that country assured the missionary that he sowed ten bushels of wheat on ten acres, and gathered more than fifty bushels from each acre.

The land of the prairies is not rich, though it produces in abundance what is called the buffalo grass.

The trees of Oregon are very large, and very beautiful. The fir-tree lifts its head among the clouds, while the cedar expends its ambition in expanding its trunk to a remarkable size. Even the black alder, which in most parts of New-England is a dimunitive tree, in Oregon affords the farmer material for twenty rails from one butt.

The farms of the missionaries were made to produce, by industry and skill, a good supply of the necessaries of the table for themselves, and for the many demands upon their hospitality which were made by the Indians and the emigrants. Those who are now settling in Oregon, and are cultivating the soil, under the superior advantages of an increased and increasing population, find it a country favorable for agricultural purposes. It is fast becoming the New-England of the Pacific shore. Though it does not yield its treasures without toil, yet it repays diligent cultivation. May its lofty mountains, its majestic rivers, and its far-extending prairies, smile upon a population of intelligent and virtuous men!

———•———

## PERPLEXITIES OF HOUSEKEEPING

Having become somewhat setttled in their new home, the missionaries very soon began to learn the peculiarities of their situation. Besides the inconveniences which were inseparable from a new country, the housekeeper found one unthought of and annoying. Indians thronged the house. They came early and often, and were seldom in a hurry to depart. They expected to be treated with something to eat, at any time. In the absence of presents of food they became morose and prejudiced. They thus increased the difficulty of performing the domestic labor of the household, as well as added to its amount. It was found necessary, therefore, in order to have a suitable degree of family quiet and rest, to fasten, at times, the doors. A well-known rap from any of its members would cause them to be opened. But to persevere in keeping the doors shut required at times no little resolution and firmness: the visitors would rattle them violently, rap at the windows, and perhaps shout for admittance: feeling no less determined to enter because they understood their calls would not then be agreeable. At one time, the housekeeper, being pressed with her domestic duties, closed her doors to pursue them without interruption. Her hands were in the dough of which she was preparing her bread. At that untimely moment an Indian chief laid his hand on the latch,—there was no admission. Was he not a chief, and should *he* be shut out, like common Indians? He was indignant. The unusual noise that he made brought the missionary toward one of the windows, her hands in no plight to receive a visitor. The window was let down at the top, a short distance. At the opening was the swarthy, angry-looking face of an uncommonly hideous-looking Indian; his feet resting on the sill and his hands on the top of the window. In a moment, and with great adroitness, he glided in at the opening, and landed at the feet of the housekeeper. A little explanation, and something to eat, removed his angry feelings, and the affair passed off without further annoyance.

Thus patience, unceasing toil, and great wisdom were necessary in order to become, in a proper degree, all things to these savage men, that they might be won to God.

———•———

## UNCOMFORTABLE NEIGHBORS

The Indians, as we have informed our readers, were not always agreeable neighbors, but of this the missionaries did not complain. They came among them *because* they were wild and untaught, that, by the blessing of God, they might become of another spirit. But they were soon made acquainted with some unwelcome neighbors, which could not be taught. The vicinity abounded with rattlesnakes. They were short, of a spotted color, slow in their movements, and easily killed. Neither was their poison so deadly as that of most of their species. The exposure of the children of the mission to them was the greatest cause of alarm they gave.

There was a large rock near the station. Under it and in its crevices lived a teeming population of these reptiles. In the cool of the evening, persons walking that way were quite sure to be startled by the sight of them.

At one time, a female missionary found one in her sleeping room. On another occasion, taking from its place a kettle, to put it on the fire, a rattlesnake was found cozily coiled up within.

The Indians have a superstitious respect for these snakes. They never kill them. They say, if they should, the "tamanas," or spirit of the murdered snake, prompts his living friends to revenge his death by biting his destroyer. The missionaries once saw an Indian occupying one part of a lodge, and a rattlesnake the other, on the most friendly terms. But they did not feel it a duty to be thus forbearing and friendly themselves; on the contrary, by every possible method, they endeavored to rid their premises of these disagreeable neighbors.

———•———

## EVENING WOLVES

Among the many perils to which the apostle was subjected were "perils in the wilderness." Those who go among savage men, to preach Christ, are often called to encounter savage beasts. Those of my readers who have read Moffat's "Southern Africa" will recollect the many narrow escapes that intrepid servant of Christ had from the lions which prowled about the habitations of those whose salvation he sought. We find, among the records from which we draw these sketches, accounts of perils in the unbroken forests through which the emigrants and missionaries had to travel. We present examples to the reader to help to make up a true picture of missionary life. True, the man of God, who counts not his life dear unto him, esteems these exposures no great cross; but the Christian, who tarries amid the securities of a gospel land, will realize, while reading of them, that they are crosses in comparison with what he endures for Christ.

The prairie and forest wolf are common animals in Oregon. As the shades of the evening gather over the forests, they come forth from their retreats, and their dismal howlings are heard in the distance. If pressed with hunger, they will attack almost any animal. When about to attack a horse, a pack of the large wolves select the fattest of the drove, set up a fearful yelling, and commence the pursuit. One after another of the pack may be left in the rear, but a few hold out in the race, until they succeed in biting the legs of the exhausted victim, and he falls, panting and mutilated, into the ferocious jaws of his pursuers.

The deer is the frequent victim of their cruelty. At one time, a deer, nearly exhausted, with his implacable enemies close at his heels, came in sight of the missionary station. As if aware of its peaceful character, he turned, leaped the inclosures, and took his place among the cattle in the yard. The wolves, with a fierce howl of disappointment, were obliged to give up their prey. The missionaries could not violate the rights of hospitality: they fed and comforted their frightened and weary guest, and, the danger being passed, bid him go in peace.

A person, for some time a member of the mission family, returned, on one occasion, from the lower settlement on the Willamette, to his own residence, fifty miles up the river, through a forest of heavy timber. The day closed, and the night overtook him in the midst of the woods. His ears were saluted by the intimidating howl of the wolves, at first seeming to come from their distant coverts, then growing louder and nearer. His horse instinctively apprehended the danger, and put forth his utmost exertions in the flight; but the pursuers gained on him rapidly, and he soon perceived that the only chance of safety was to abandon his horse, and ascend a tree. This he did with all expedition, taking his saddle with him, and tying his horse at the foot, — scarcely daring to hope that he would escape the hungry jaws of the savage beasts. Putting his saddle astride an extended limb, he sat upon it, and lashed himself to the body of the tree. Looking around, the moment he began to feel himself secure, for some means of protecting his horse, he found he had left his gun at the bottom of the tree.

The wolves, however, feared to approach, or were providentially attracted by some more easy prey. They left the missionary to watch away the tedious night, which he did in no very quiet mood; and descended at the approach of day, and pursued his journey.

At another time this same brother was in more imminent danger. He was on foot, and being overtaken by the darkness in the forest, the wolves were soon in hot pursuit. He ran with his utmost speed, calling aloud for help. He heard the panting of his hungry enemies, just behind; but his call had alarmed the inmates of a house, fortunately near. The only one at hand, to run to his rescue, was a woman, who, in her haste, seized a cooper's compass, and sallied forth to his assistance. The light, probably, of a human habitation, more than the woman, intimidated the wolves, and they retired. Thus was the kind providence of God again apparent in the preservation of his servant.

We know that such exposures are no more than men endure to gratify a spirit of adventure, or to satisfy a thirst for gold; but when they are voluntarily borne, "in weariness and painfulness, in watchings often, in hunger and thirst, in cold and nakedness," "not for filthy lucre's sake, but of a ready mind," it becomes a matter of deep interest to Christians. We follow the servant of God through such scenes, and believe that his trials will turn out, in God's overruling providence, to the furtherance of the gospel.

———•———

## EMIGRANTS TO OREGON

The station of our missionaries lay in the traveled route from the United States to the Willamette Valley. Every year the number of emigrants became larger, and their demands upon the hospitality and assistance of the missionaries greater. In 1843, wagons, for the first time, were used through the whole distance. Previously they had been left at the Rocky Mountains. The first successful experiment to bring them further was made by the lamented Dr. Whitman, a missionary of the American Board. During that year, three thousand persons passed over this route to the Pacific shore. They consisted of men, women, and children—from the old man to the infant born on the way. In one family were eight children. They had started from their former home in fine health and spirits, for a new home, yet to be prepared in the forests of the Willamette Valley. The parents were taken sick upon the road, died, and were laid in rude graves by their companions in travel. The orphaned children were left to the compassion of strangers to aid them in performing the yet difficult and long journey. The watchful providence of Him who will not let the raven cry in vain, and whose ear is ever open to the orphan's prayer, was over them. Dr. Whitman took them into his own family, and became to them a father and religious teacher.

The toil and privations of the overland route were, at this time, very great. During one year twenty died. When these emigrants arrived at the missionary station, they were, of course, greatly rejoiced to behold, after having been familiar so long with nothing but Indian encampments, the habitation of white men. They were often very destitute, and, in most cases, taxed heavily the kindness of their Christian friends, who were not by any means abundantly supplied with the conveniences or even the necessities of life. But they made great exertions, toiling hard early and late, and sacrificing often their own little comforts, to aid the suffering.

The year 1846 brought with it incidents, in connection with the emigrants, which made a deep impression on the minds of the missionaries. One party, of two hundred and twenty-five wagons, engaged a man as a guide who had been a trapper in the Rocky Mountains, and pretended to possess great knowledge of the country. It was subsequently supposed that he was hired, by some persons interested, to guide them to the head waters of the Willamette, far away from their purposed place of settlement. Professing to lead them through a new and nearer route, they became entangled in the forest, lost their way, exhausted their provisions, so as to be driven to the necessity of killing cattle which were worn down with labor and disease; this brought on fever, and many of them died. The survivors arrived at the mission station, subjects of unspeakable distress. Some were sick, and ready to die; others bore, with exhausted steps, the corpses of deceased friends. One father had left, in a lonely grave, his eldest son, and brought the body of another dear child, who had just died, to be interred with Christian rites and the sympathy of Christian men. The mother of these children was, in the mean time, borne along by her grief-oppressed husband upon a bed of extreme sickness and pain. She, it is believed, lived to see a comfortable home reared on the banks of the Willamette; but a home made sad by the absence of those who were to have been its lights, and the source of parental pride and happiness. Such is life; but such is *not* heaven, where tears shall never flow, because sin can never enter.

Another case in this company was peculiarly afflicting. A husband buried, after he arrived at the mission, his wife and infant child. The mother was a worthy member of the Methodist Church, and died in great peace.

These circumstances of course brought a great addition to the responsibility and labor of our missionaries. While they did all they could for the *bodies* of the sufferers, they were enabled also to administer to the healing of their souls, and to sow some precious seed, which they trust, under the Holy Spirit, bore fruit unto eternal life.

The moral influence of the emigrants upon the Indians was generally very bad, rendering more difficult all exertions to bring them under the influence of Christianity. The white men, usually well armed, and in considerable companies, were too often oppressive and exacting of the red men, who, destitute and ignorant, were disposed to steal on every favorable occasion. In one case, a notorious gambler and his associates had their horses stolen by two Indians. They pursued, overtook them, and, having first recovered the horses, killed the thieves. These cases of cruelty, with the repeated instances of fraud practiced upon them by the white men, were no small hinderance to the introduction of the gospel among these heathen. Yet did the missionaries not despair. The Spirit of God was their ground of hope. He could and did cause the wronged red man to feel his enlightening power, though this truth was made to appear as a lie, in the character of those who had received most freely his gracious influence.

The toils occasioned by the circumstances we have above narrated brought one of the missionary family upon a bed of severe sickness. Yet how could such self-destroying labor have been avoided? Truly, a martyr's crown must be theirs who thus fall! How much better thus to *die* than to live in ease amid the luxuries of the Church in Christian lands, never offering a cup of cold water even to Christ, in the person of his suffering children!

———•———

## ADROIT BEGGARS

One of the first sources of trial to the missionary, among the Indians, is their persevering and teasing spirit of begging. Scarcely were our friends settled in their new home when they had a trial of this kind; and, as it was a good example of what was constantly occurring, we present it as an illustration of the Indian character in this respect.

A large, muscular man, well able to hunt game, to fish, to fell trees, to clear land, or in almost any way to support himself and family by honest labor, appeared at the mission house, one morning, *early*, and first requested a breakfast. This was the practice of the beggars. His air was very gracious, mixed with the ludicrously solemn.

Having satisfied his appetite, he commenced: "O, Mr. B______, I no come here for nothing,—business very great. I come a great ways on purpose." Then standing erect, and exhibiting a miserable blanket, his only covering, when perhaps he had left a good supply of clothing at home, he would exclaim, "See, me no got coat," at the same time grasping his brawny arm in his hand; "and me no got pants," showing his uncovered leg. "Me poor, O, very poor!" Then, with admirable tact and feigned sincerity, he began to flatter: "Mr. B______, you are a *man* — a *great* man. You are a man of *great heart*. You are a *great chief*. I hear of your greatness and generosity before you arrive in this country. You are greater and better than all the other missionaries. You love poor Indian, and have come to do them good; and I have come to get my wants supplied."

An entire outfit was the object of his first effort; but he was prepared to recede somewhat from the extent of his demand. Not meeting with a favorable response, he began to say, "A coat, only a coat, — a pair of pants, — a vest." Again, measuring his request by the amount of encouragement, he pleaded for a handkerchief or a pair of socks. Not succeeding with the husband, he turned to the wife: "My wife tell me to tell you she want a dress;" and moderating his demand in the same way, he finally urged his suit for a dress for the poor little child, whose clothes "are bad, O, very bad!"

He was at last pacified in some measure with a small piece of soap and a few pieces of sewing thread. He then went to the other missionary, to go over the same story, — complaining that Mr. B______ was "mean." He had "a little heart, — O, a very small heart, no bigger than a flea!"

Such was the constant habit of these untaught savages. The means of the missionaries, at this period especially, even for supplying their own wants, were limited, and they possessed but very little to bestow in charity. But even if they had had more, their judgment forbade them answering such calls, which grew out of an idle desire to obtain, rather than from necessity. The missionaries aimed rather to teach them habits of industry, by which they could supply their own wants. But it required much patience to bear with their importunity, and to refuse, and yet not offend so as to prejudice them against the gospel.

---

### TREATMENT OF THE SICK

Indian tradition says that "Talipaz," that is the "Prairie Wolf," was the creator of all things. "Yes," the Indians exclaim, "he made the Columbia, and all the rivers, — the mountains, the forests, the buffalo, and even the Indians. From his *blood* came the Cayuse; from his *heart* came the Lion Hearted tribe; from his *arm* the Chenwook; and from various parts of his body came all the tribes." It is not strange, therefore, that even now they treat Talipaz with much tenderness. He may come and go, if he does not attack them, without molestation: even their dogs, which much resemble the wolf, being doubtless possessed of some wolf blood, they treat with great respect, on account of their supposed relationship to Talipaz.

When a young man wishes to become distinguished, he goes out at night,—perhaps some night when the clouds overhang the sky,—and an awful mystery seems to enshroud the object of his adventure. He claims to meet either Talipaz or his spirit. Sometimes he says, "Tamanawas," that is, a moving spirit of power, "came upon me." He now knows what is to befall him, or he vainly thinks, in his superstition, he knows more than common mortals. He claims to be a great "medicine man;" and, strange enough, his people allow his claim!

"William," said the missionary to an unusually intelligent boy of the mission family, "why do your people believe that the 'medicine men' can kill or cure, just as they please?"

"O, they *can*," answered William, with a look of immovable gravity; "certainly they can."

"How can it be, William?"

"O, Tamanawas has given them the power. Now, if you give the great medicine man, Kladioula, two blankets, and say, 'Kill Tumeocool,' he will do it."

"Yes," said the teacher, "he may tomahawk or shoot him."

"Ah, no; he will not go near him: may be he will not see him. By and by Tumeocool feels sick, O, *very* sick; then he lays down, and pretty soon Tumeocool is dead, *dead*;" and he emphasized the last word in a way which showed that, to his mind, there were no doubts about it.

"Do not the 'medicines' pretend this, to *cheat* the poor Indians?" said the missionary; "and to cause them to fear them, that they may more easily get their blankets and guns?"

"Ah no!" said William, thoughtfully; "they are true medicines."

So powerfully does ignorance keep the red man a slave to imposition.

Having shown the source of the pretended power of the Indian doctors, we will now illustrate, by a few interesting facts, the manner in which they treat the sick.

**The Indian Doctor**

Having, for some time, heard much of the management of the imposters, but never having seen for themselves, our missionaries went, one day, to the lodge of a sick man, who had sent for a "medicine," who was already there. After an examination, he shook his head, and said, dolefully, "Sick, very sick. Tamanawas is destroying your vitals." Then looking meaningly around, he added, "Of what use are your blankets, your guns, and your horses? — you die soon. *Give me* three blankets, then I kill Tamanawas, and you get well."

The appeal, as usual, succeeded, and the blankets being promised, the conjurer commenced his demoniac ceremony. The sick man's friends were seated on one side of the lodge, with a board before them, upon which they commenced beating, and joining with the doctor in a low, indescribable wail; while he, upon his knees, was throwing his body into all manner of contortions. He was without clothes, except a narrow strip of cloth about his loins, and seemed prepared for a desperate struggle. Suddenly throwing himself upon the sick man, he commenced sucking at the pit of his stomach, as if he would devour instead of cure; then starting off a little distance, he gave a desperate bound upon him. Now commenced a frantic struggle, as if the Tamanawas was contending hard for the mastery, while the conjurer feigned an impossibility of extricating himself. Two strong men went to his relief, and removed him by force. Breaking away from them, he sprang for some water, into which he thrust his closed hand, which contained the Tamanawas, wrested from the sick man, and now drowned.

The missionaries looked in vain to see anything, either in his hand or in the water. He now skrieked at the top of his voice, and his friends shouted in triumph, and proclaimed the victory complete.

Though thus successful, in their own estimation, in this first effort, the same ceremony was performed over this man every day, for six months; and he finally lived, in spite of the desperate remedy.

If the sick man recovered, the doctor retains his fee; but if he dies it is returned, and the medicine man is fortunate if his life is not taken by the friends of the deceased. In fact, the Indians make a kind of virtue of killing their doctors, so that but few assume this character.

The following illustration of this practice of murder occurred at the Dalls mission station. The parties were known to the missionaries. A neighbor fell into a rapid decline, probably a quick consumption, and died. His friends, after his burial, began to throw the responsibility of his death upon an old doctor, on the other side of the Columbia, though he had not even seen the deceased man. As there is no reason nor compassion in ignorance and superstition, one of the friends of the deceased, urged on by blind passion, took his gun, crossed the river, shot the unoffending man in his wigwam, and returned, boasting of his foul deed.

Though the ceremony above described is the principal mode adopted by the Indians in their medical practice, yet it is not the only one. They have a common and curious kind of *preventive* as well as cure of sickness. In every village there is, at least, one *sweating oven*. They excavate a large hole in the side of a hill, and in it bend poles over, in the shape of an oven, covering the poles with mats, and then with earth. A pile of stones is gathered near the mouth of the oven, over which a fire is kept burning until they are hot. These stones they take with them into the oven. Having shut themselves in, they pour water upon the stones, thus producing a steam. They are soon almost suffocated with heat and vapor, and of course perspire very freely. After remaining in the oven as long as nature will possibly suffer such treatment, they break away from their place of suffocation, and plunge into cold water.

How must the heart of every Christian, and especially of every Sunday-school convert, yearn to point such ignorant beings to the true Physician, who, while he heals the heart of its disease of sin, brings such light to the mind, that better care is taken of the mortal body! As these Indians came under the instruction of the missionaries, in the same degree they broke away from confidence in these poor physicians, and adopted more reasonable remedies.

Missionaries, to some extent, became the medical advisers of the Indians, so far as they were permitted to do so; and by this means obtained often a favorable influence over them. But to advise for *such* patients, having habits so peculiar, and possessing so little judgment in taking medicine, was no pleasant task. They would come to the mission, and say, "Friend, I have come to you for relief. I am sick: my stomach is dark, and screwed up. You are a wise man. Come, friend, get me well."

The most simple medicine was given. Often some little device, to divert them to a simple mode of living for a few days, would remove a serious illness. In a case like the above, where the patient was known to be living on indigestible, greasy food, a bunch of lettuce was given, with great gravity, as an excellent medicine. It operated admirably, and the patient was loud in his praises of both the medicine and the doctor. At another time the case was much more serious, but resulted, by the blessing of God, equally well. An Indian came dashing up to the mission house, —his horse panting with hard riding. "O, Mr. B______," he exclaimed, "I have come twenty-five miles! You are very wise. I have come for help. One of our women has been bitten by a rattlesnake. I have come to get a cure."

Here was a critical case. Something must be done promptly. The missionary had heard that the common onion, applied raw to the bitten part, was an effective remedy. A dangerous medicine could not be used under such circumstances, and this seemed the only resort. It was sent by the messenger, who returned in furious haste.

Several weeks passed before he came again. One day he entered the mission house, and exclaimed, "O, you great doctor! My heart is large toward you! You are wise, O, *very* wise! Ah, that medicine cure, —woman, she get well right off!"

## SICKNESS, FUNERAL CEREMONIES, AND BURIAL OF THE DEAD

When an Indian is taken sick, his family consult his friends immediately. If an Indian doctor is called, they are expected to assist. The sick man generally dreads this expedient, as the patients of these famous practitioners very commonly die, and are never cured by *their means*. If the friends undertake the case themselves, more common sense is used. The most comfortable bed possible is made, which usually consists of a little dried grass, a mat, and a buffalo skin, laid in a corner of the wigwam. If the sick person be a slave, he is abandoned altogether. If not a slave, yet, if he grows worse, he will be much or altogether neglected, until death interposes, and closes the scene.

Now commences a most dismal howling, in lamentation for the dead, which lasts often seven days, — the length of time being determined, somewhat, by their regard for the deceased. Women are the chief mourners, and are often hired for this purpose. Their mourning is frequently like that of the Israelites for Jacob, at the threshing-floor of Atad, "a grievous and bitter mourning."

As soon as the breath leaves the body, the corpse is bound up, by those accustomed to the business, in a blanket, or skin, and the neighbors and friends make presents to the relatives of the deceased, of beads, shells, and sometimes of more valuable articles, depositing them on the corpse. A few of the Indians, through the influence of the example of the whites, bury their dead after the fashion of civilized communities. The Dalls Indians carried their deceased friends to an island in the Columbia River. It consists of a rocky ledge, in which no graves can be dug. They there built rude houses, and in them deposited the bodies, leaving them to waste away, much exposed, necessarily, to the air. When the bones are bleached and bare, they pile them in one indiscriminate heap. The aspect of this place is truly dismal, and speaks mournfully of the necessity of the correcting influence of the gospel, by which the deed might be laid beneath the ground, in hope of a glorious resurrection.

After the ceremony of placing the corpse in its resting place is over, the immediate friends of the deceased retire to a secluded spot, where water can be freely obtained; and for a number of days they give themselves up to a purifying process, washing and rubbing themselves as if to remove some infection. This done, they are then ready to return to contact with society. None can fail to see in this ceremony, as well as that of mourning, a resemblance to Jewish customs. A scrupulous division of the property of the departed among the surviving friends is an item belonging to the Indian customs, in connection with the funeral, which is never omitted.

## THE INDIAN NATIONAL DANCE

Most nations have their yearly holidays, and their peculiar manner of celebrating them. The well-known "Thanksgiving," which for a long time was considered a New-England festival, has become almost national. How pleasant is the meeting of friends on that day! How pleasing the associations of cheerful homes and well-spread tables! Especially, how grateful to the Christian mind the religious service in God's house! The Indians of Oregon have a yearly holiday, as we may call it; but its celebration is that of heathenism, and not of civilization and Christianity.

In several successive seasons the missionaries had noticed in the month of December, that a noise, as of a peculiar pounding and singing, proceeded from the Indian villages. Of this they had thought but little, as the noise of carousings was so frequent in that place. But its regular occurence in December induced inquiries, which resulted in their first information concerning the Indians' yearly national dance. Invited by some Indian friends, the missionary entered the lodge set apart for the performance. It was prepared by the erection of rough apartments for the spectators, from which the performance could be seen. A dried elk skin was stretched at the head of the room, on which the dancers performed, one at a time. The first dancer was a middle-aged man, who came upon the stand dressed with only a sheet around his waist, and a belt with a pistol at his side. He commenced with a low, singing tone, in which his Indian audience joined. His dancing consisted in violent twistings and wrenchings of his body, without at any time lifting his feet from the platform. This exercise he continued for half an hour, or more, occasionally changing the time of his song, if it might so be called, and distributing, during the performance, among his audience, beads, dressed dear skin, flax, &c. This custom of the dancers paying the people who consent to witness their performance is known, we presume, only to the Indians; but we suggest whether it is not more reasonable than for the audience to *pay the dancers?*

After this performer had retired, and the audience were in silent expectation of another, a large, hideous-looking Indian plunged through the aperture in the roof of the building, out of which the smoke escaped, and, with one leap, landed upon the elk skin. His face and nearly naked body were smeared with blood. He began with a low, gutteral tone, increasing in loudness as he proceeded in his dance, which, as before, consisted in contortions of the body. When he was about half through, one of his friends seized a small dog, doubtless procured for the purpose, and attempted to take its life by thrice thrusting it into the fire. Not succeeding in this cruel mode of killing the animal, it was cut open, and the blood—for which it had been killed—was handed in a vessel to the dancer, who eagerly drank it, meaning to say to his audience, by the clotted blood upon his body, and the blood taken within, that he was a man of blood, thus gloring in his shame.

Disgusted at the sight, the missionary hastily left the building, and, with a heavy heart, hurried to his own quiet home.

————•————

## INDIAN SLAVERY

As in Africa, so in our Western Territories, the different native tribes make war upon each other, and reduce their captives to slavery. It does not appear, however, that the Indians, like Africans, make war for the *purpose* of making slaves. Slavery with them is only one of the consequences of their quarrels. The features of the system, as we are about to describe them, have reference particularly to the tribes of Western Oregon. The Shastas and Klameths, in the southern districts, have been at enmity for a long time. In their predatory incursions upon each other, they seize upon defenseless women and children, and bear them away into captivity. In some cases the males are enslaved, but the difficulty of retaining men as property prevents this result from frequent occurrence.

These slaves are purchased by the more northern tribes. A horse, or six beaver skins, or two blankets, or a pair of pantaloons and a vest, will purchase a slave. None but some one of the native tribes are ever thus held in bondage.

But war, though the *usual*, is not the *only* means of making slaves. The Indians have a violent passion for gambling. It is nearly as characteristic and as strong as their love or ardent spirit. When therefore, they have nothing else to stake, they gamble away their liberty; beginning with an arm or a leg, they risk limb after limb, until the whole man is put into the venture, to be given up to bondage for a specified time, or, in some extreme cases, for life.

The service to which the slaves are subjected is the most menial. They dress the food taken in the chase or in fishing, draw water, and provide wood for the fire. Their food is course and scanty, even more so than that of their masters. They go almost destitute of clothing. When they are sick they are frequently left wholly uncared for, — nourishment not even being provided them; and thus they die alone, with disease and starvation. The house where they die is pulled down, the premises forsaken, and the body left unburied.

The missionaries once saw a poor slave boy, who was sick, taken by his master from the lodge, and laid upon a mat, in a hole dug for the purpose, so that he might thus die in his grave!

These religious teachers were the means of preventing, in many cases, such cruelty; and by making the dark mind of the Indian understand the law of love, they were the instruments of the abolition, in a measure, of this system of slavery.

Occasionally the enslaved men would, by energy of character very rare among the Indians, purchase their freedom. A doctor of some note, known to the missionaries, was from his boyhood enslaved. Being shrewd, and recommending himself by his good conduct, he became free and influential.

———◆———

## RANSOM

The Indian, Sinimhe, had a son who was taken suddenly ill. He was dear to his father, and every means was used to save him that parental affection could devise, guided, alas, by no skillful hand! The boy died, and the father's heart was deeply wounded. He mourned for him with howlings and other heathen expressions of sorrow. He determined that the burial should be accompanied by the greatest possible respect for the remains of his departed son. In his family was a slave, a boy eight or ten years of age, a great favorite of the deceased, and his affectionate attendant in his last hours. Him the father commanded to go with the procession to the sepulcher. When there, he bound him, placed him in the tomb, with his face downward, and confined him, with strong cords, to the corpse of his son! The struggles and entreaties of the slave were unheeded: the place of burial was closed, and the mourners returned to their homes.

Toward night of the same day, Yaquator, an attendant upon the sad scene, came to the family of the missionary. He began to relate, pensively, the tale of the late sickness and death, in language something as follows: "Sinimhe, he feel sorry, *very* sorry, — sorry *here*," laying his hand upon his heart. "They make much mourning, — a *great* cry, O, a *very great* cry! They bury with him much things, — they bury *slave* with him. O, Sinimhe love him a great, *great* love!"

At the last expressions the attention and interest of the missionary family were intensely excited.

"A *slave* buried! — who? where?"

"O, a *slave* buried, sure," replied the Indian, becoming more quiet, seeing the feeling his message had excited, and seemed to give to the affair an air of trifling importance.

But not such were the feelings of the Christian family. They urged him to go instantly, and obtain his immediate relief; and, to give emphasis to their entreaties, they intimated that, if it were not done, Dr. M'Laughlin should know of the cruel act.

Yaquator carried this message to other Indians concerned, and they were intimidated; but they could not be persuaded to visit the grave that night. It was some distance off, and their superstitious dread of the place of the dead, and of him who, though now living, dwelt there was not easily overcome. The next morning, however, the missionaries succeeded in obtaining his release. His limbs were swollen, and much cut by the cords and his struggles to get free. He was unable, for awhile, to stand. He was taken to the mission house, (the Indian superstition keeping them aloof from him,) and carefully washed and clothed, for he had been entombed naked. The mission boys for some time avoided him. In two weeks he was nearly recovered, and became communicative and sprightly. He said he slept none during that terrible night, but watched, and *listened to the singing of the dead.**

His deliverers gave him the appropriate name of Ransom. He remained for some time under their watch-care.

———•———

## THE INDIAN MODE OF REMOVAL

The Indians, especially in the middle and upper country, where they follow the chase for a living, are exceedingly fond of horses. These animals they own often in large numbers. The chief selects from four to ten of the best for his own use.

When a company are about to remove, the *women* take down the lodge; and if it be covered with skins, as is often the case, it is packed upon horses, trained for that purpose. The poles are attached at one end to each side of the saddle, and the other end is permitted to drag upon the ground. Clothing, lodge-covering, buffalo robes, and the scanty articles of housekeeping, are packed upon other horses.

Each child, if old enough to ride alone, has a horse; if not, they ride behind the mother; or, if a mere infant, it is often slung to a horse by itself, and the horse turned loose among the company. The women take charge of the horses carrying *burdens*, and the men take charge of the others.

Thus equipped, they move from place to place. Their removals are generally in the winter. When they reach their place of destination, the *women* clear away the snow, prepare the ground, and set up the lodge; the men sitting upon their horses, or squatting about the fire, until their houses are made ready to be occupied.

The lower country Indians do not usually have skin lodges; but their winter houses, being partly under ground, are covered with boards. These they take down in the spring, bury the boards in the excavation in which they have lived, and construct a summer, traveling lodge of a kind of rush, or coarse grass. These they easily transfer, as we have described, from place to place, on their horses.

* It is a common notion among the Indians, that the dead may be heard to sing in the places of burial.

What would these sons of the forest say or think, if they were at once to exchange their tedious mode of travel for a railroad car, moving at the rate of thirty miles an hour?

———•———

## FLATTENING INFANTS' HEADS

So far as our missionaries' knowledge extends, the tribes which flatten their heads and pierce their noses and ears are the Chenooks, Walla-Wallas, Klickatats, Callapooyahs, and some others, mostly in lower Oregon. It is singular that the so called Flatheads and Nez Perces (Pierced Noses) neither flatten their heads nor pierce their noses.

The process of flattening the head of the infant is as follows. Soon after the child is born, a board is prepared, of a proper length, wider at the head than foot; upon the edge of this board a narrow piece of skin is fastened, with loop-holes at short distances. Upon this board they lay grass, skin, or fur. The "tumchasas," or cradle, is then complete. Upon this the infant is laid. The mother confines closely its feet, legs, and body, with cords, placing the little arms snugly by its side. A wide strip of skin is passed across the head, and lashed to the board; and the suffering babe is left, with the poor privilege of *seeing* and breathing, if it can. In this position it is kept from twelve to eighteen hours each day, during the first year or more. Their eyes are started frightfully from their heads, and multitudes of them die in this cruel process. A few survive, with their heads so exceedingly flattened as nearly to form an edge at the top. The people of these tribes, more especially the chiefs, are very vain of their flat heads.

———•———

## AN INDIAN MARRIAGE

The Christian religion has sanctified the marriage relation, and made sacred the names of "husband" and "wife." In the dark corners of the earth, where are the habitations of cruelty, man is generally the oppressive master, and woman the trembling slave. The marriage ceremony is a disgusting mockery, and the *wife* is regarded as such only so long as she shall please her fickle lord. In proportion as Bible truth has prevailed, has the rite of marriage been made interesting and solemn. In the Eastern countries, in the Saviour's time, and even at the present day, nuptial rites are strikingly beautiful. From these the Saviour drew many impressive illustrations of religious doctrines. The reader will recollect his reference to the midnight processions, and the cry, "The bridegroom cometh,"—the shutting of the door of admittance to the feast, and the lamentations of those forbidden to enter.

The marriage occasions of our own Christian land are distinctly impressed upon the minds of my youthful readers. We will now present to them a heathen mode of celebrating marriage. It must be borne in mind that the heathen referred to had long been under the ameliorating influence of some form of Christian civilization, and therefore these ceremonies are less repulsive than those of other heathens.

In the case selected as an illustration of our subject, the consent of each party had be obtained. The object now was to confirm the engagement, and to constitute the parties husband and wife. The bridegroom was a young man, called, by the missionaries, Joseph, who had lived in an American friend's family.

The ceremony commenced with the presentation, by Joseph, to the bride, of five horses. The number varies from two to twenty, according to the wealth or generosity of the bridegroom. They are brought to the door of the bride, and left without remark. As these gifts are not regarded as purchase money, but as expressions of earnestness in the matter, Joseph waited for an expression from his espoused in return. After a little delay, an old man, the crier, came toward the bridegroom, with a stick hoisted in the air, to which was attached a long string of large beads, one end of which he held in his hand: he muttered, as he came, something which was understood to mean, "Look, look! This for one horse!" In like manner, strings of various kinds of shells were presented, and the acceptance of each horse was thus acknowledged.

The next step was taken by a company of fifteen young women, friends of the bride, who arranged themselves in rows of three each,—the whole procession being connected by a string of beads. They thus marched toward the bridegroom's

**An Indian Wedding**

29

residence, chanting merrily as they went, and deposited them before him, receiving some small articles in return, which they coolly appropriated to their own especial use.

The next step the missionaries did not consider very complimentary to the bride, but such was the custom. Joseph sent his mother and sister, with combs and tallow, to put the espoused's hair in a bridal condition. After they had performed the duty intrusted them, they left the tallow and combs in her possession, as an intimation, perhaps, that it would be well for her and her friends to continue to use them.

Next came the feast, which was served up at the bride's house, to the bridegroom and his friends only. It consisted of dried salmon and cammas-root, mixed with salmon oil, presented by the bride on small mats, made for the occasion.

Joseph and his friends having satisfied their appetites, returned to his house, carrying the remains of the feast and the mats with them. They soon returned, each with a back-load of wood, for the bride's father; and thus ended the ceremony. They were now pronounced, "*by custom*," husband and wife; to live with each other, alas! *not* "according to God's most holy ordinance of matrimony," but according to the heathen notions of the husband, who might put his wife away for "every cause;" or take to himself, at will, another, to share with her his affections and commands.

---

### THE WAR SPIRIT

It is a fact long known to the whites that the red men, of every part of our country, are rapidly fading away. Their bad habits of living are the principal cause, no doubt; but their bloody wars against each other have a great influence in securing this result. It is especially so in Oregon. Since the missionaries have lived among them, their warlike spirit has, in some measure, been subdued; but, even now, the more numerous and stronger tribes oppress the weaker. The Nez Perces and Cayuses, at one time, very much annoyed the Wascapams, making large demands upon them, so that they fled for refuge to dens and caves.

The Nez Perces and Cayuses were accustomed to visit our missionaries, when on their yearly excursions. It was on one of these visits that the missionaries were *treated* with an exhibition of their manner of engaging in battle. It was not exactly a war-dance, but was attended by those savage yells and howlings which accompany their dances.

They first announced their approach to the station by firing their guns, by drumming, and by terrific war-songs. They were mounted on horses, strangely decorated. From the head of one streamed the hair of the scalp of a Blackfoot Indian; from another, the hideous scalp of a buffalo, — the horns still protruding. Their riders were not less fantastically dressed. All available ornament, and different-colored clothes, were laid under contribution, — the garment, in some instances, trailing to the ground. They came on with furious prancing and reckless disorder, yelling and singing as they came. A part alighted near the mission house, and danced, yelled, and drummed, much, doubtless, to *their own* gratification. One of the chiefs then entered the house, to assure the inmates of their peaceful purposes; an assurance not altogether unnecessary, we should think, after the exhibition of so much of the spirit of war. They only wished to show them, he said, how they prepared for battle.

The men, having finished this performance, loitered about the settlement, expecting presents; while their *wives* were engaged in erecting their lodges, for they had come intending to spend some months at the station.

How hateful is the spirit of war, wherever it is seen, or by whomsoever exhibited, whether in the savage warwhoop or the stirring tones of the bugle! It is to subdue this spirit, and make men love one another, that the gospel is preached, bearing "glad tidings of great joy," and proclaiming, "Peace on earth, and good will to men." So far as it shall have willing ears, and obedient hearts, whether in savage or in Christian lands, the howlings of the Indian, and the martial music of the soldier, in preparation for bloody conflict with their fellow-men, will give way to the joyful shout, from "a great multitude, whom no man can number, saying, Alleluia, for the Lord God Omnipotent reigneth." Who would not be engaged, with all the means in his power, to secure this glorious reign of the King of peace?

---

### THE TENDER MERCY OF HEATHENISM

It cannot be denied that heathen parents have generally some of the affection which belongs to that parental relation. They even, at times, exhibit a frantic fondness for their offspring: but, being "without God," their passions are not chastened, nor rightly directed. They often are impelled to deeds, by the darkness of their minds, which stifle all the tender sympathies of their nature, and appear truly "without natural affection." Such was the case with Homaz, a brave and distinguished Wascapam. His tribe regarded him as a chief; and the missionaries discovered in him more than usual tact and ability in discussing many subjects of interest. This, in many respects, noble savage had an infant child. The little babe the missionaries thought possessed unusual beauty and attractiveness, and its mother, though an Indian, seemed to think so too. But, like many infants it cried much. This disturbed the father. Shaking his head, he would say, "*Wrong,* — bad, very bad," meaning that there was something very wrong about the child. The Christian father would have at once referred it to a slight sickness, or passed it by altogether: but the darkened mind of this heathen must seek a more mysterious reason. "It is," said he, "because I went into the steam-oven, a few days before its birth. Its heart is, therefore, like a steam-oven, and it *must not* live." Such was his reasoning, and he determined to destroy his child, probably thinking to rid the child of pain and himself of the annoyance of its crying.

Of this purpose the missionary, of course, knew nothing, but providentially called at the lodge of Homaz, to converse with him concerning the cross of Christ. The medicine man was present, and Homaz was silent and sullen. The missionary engaged in conversation with the father, while the doctor squatted down by the mother, who held the infant in her arms. Suddenly, the mother gave a piercing shriek, the doctor gave a savage yell, and the babe gasped convulsively, and died! The doctor, with a terrible grasp, had strangled the child in its mother's arms. The father remained unmoved, coolly surveying the scene; too plainly showing that *he* had planned the murder.

It was the work of a moment, and the Christian teacher could only remonstrate against such heart-rending deeds, in the name of Jesus, who took little children up in his arms, and blessed them.

The poor mother was overwhelmed with affliction; she showed her grief by mournful wailings. The missionary tried to teach her that "of such is the kingdom of heaven."

Let us pity and pray for these murderers, that the light of the gospel may take away their hearts of stone, and give them the love that suffereth long, and is kind. Sincerely grateful should the Sabbath-school children be, that their parents were not exposed to the darkness of the savage, whose tender mercies are cruel.

---

## CAMP-MEETING

Those means of grace denominated the class-meeting, the love-feast, and the camp-meeting, were used by the missionaries among the Indians with God's special blessing. Though the weekly class might be held in an humble hut, the love-feast in a place of rude accommodations, and the camp-meeting with far less outward conveniences than those of Christian lands, yet God, whose peculiar habitation is with the lowly, blessed these means.

The first camp-meeting that our missionaries held was in October, 1841. The spot selected was a clean prairie, about three miles from the Dalles station. Peculiar feelings were inspired by the novel scene. About thirty brush tents, erected by the Indians, encircled the ground. No seats were necessary for the sons of the forest, who sometimes call the earth their mother, and prefer to rest upon her bosom. Frequently, when seats are prepared for them, in other places, they sit upon them for awhile, restless and dissatisfied, and then, slipping down between them, take a more satisfactory position upon the ground. Thus a congregation, seated at the commencement of a service, would be upon the ground at its close.

At this meeting no pulpit stand was prepared; the preacher, while standing, being sufficiently elevated above his audience. About five hundred Indians were assembled. The following order of exercises was adopted, and obeyed cheerfully and promptly: all seemed to be interested. At six o'clock, A.M., prayer-meeting in the tents; seven o'clock, secret prayer, at which time many could be seen directing their steps, in different directions, or private supplication. The breakfast hour was eight o'clock; and at ten all were to assemble upon the prairie to hear preaching; after which an hour was spent in private devotion again. Then another sermon was preached, followed, after a short intermission, by a frugal dinner. Next in order was preaching, and social and private prayer, until the evening meal. The day was closed with prayer and exhortation, in the tents.

Thus the time passed pleasantly and profitably until the Sabbath, which was a day of extraordinary interests. Brother J. Lee baptized one hundred and thirty persons, and administered the sacrament to over four hundred, — mostly adults. Glorious were the manifestations of the divine power! Shouts of praise ascended from hundreds of new-born souls; and experienced believers rejoiced in God's quickening grace. Even the unyielding sinner was astonished, and his gainsaying was stopped. A new sound had broke forth in this wilderness, — its solitary places were made glad. Often the coveted laborers exclaimed, "O that the Christian friends of our native land were here, to witness the work of grace on the hearts of the Indians."

After the meeting closed, the native converts continued to give evidence of a genuine change of heart. They needed, it is true, a constant watch-care, persevering and patient instruction, and sometimes the faithful Christian reproof. It must be remembered they were but recently in heathen darkness, and were still surrounded with pagan superstitions. Their teachers, therefore, rejoiced over them with trembling, and mourned, as a parent for a prodigal child, when they went astray. They had the happiness of seeing many of them continue steadfast in the faith, and die in hope of a glorious immortality.

The following spring, another camp-meeting was held. Much prayer had been offered, that God would own this assembling in the grove, — that he would revive the fainting, arouse the stupid, convict the unawakened, and sanctify believers. The Head of the Church heard, and answered. As the missionary passed from tent to tent, instruction and exhorting, his heart was rejoiced by the prayer and praise of the Indian converts. One would exclaim, "I am happy, happy; the Holy Spirit given to me is like food to my soul!" Another said, "When I came here my heart was *po-na-ni-cow,—dark, dark!* When I prayed my heart was hard, like a stone. I prayed again and again, and I felt better; and now "—putting his hand upon his heart—"it is all light *here*,—all joy in the Lord."

Some weeks afterward the missionary writes: "The good work is still going on. We hold meetings with the Indians dayly. They weep and pray,—weep, and rejoice with joy unspeakable. They are full, and rejoice from the heart. *Our* hearts are frequently melted, and we have a shout of a King in the camp.

"When we are having our services in English, for the more immediate benefit of our little circle, the Indian converts will come in, and, although they do not understand our language, yet they catch the spirit of our devotions, and rejoice with us."

Such were some of the features of the camp-meetings among the red men,—such the blessed fruits. Upon them the missionary looks back, delighting to ponder upon the goodness of God; and he is prompted to look forward in joyful expectation, that he will meet in heaven those who shall say, "There and then were we made heirs of this glorious inheritance."

———•———

ERUPTION OF MOUNT ST. HELENS, AND A PEAK OF THE PRESIDENT'S RANGE

On a pleasant evening, in the month of November, 1843, the missionaries at the Dalles were favored with a visit from some of their friends from the Willamette Valley. Among the company was the celebrated Tom M'Kay, who was the terror of all the upper country Indians. In earlier days he had been sent, by the Hudson's Bay Company, to punish them for various misdemeanors. So energetically had this hardy pioneer performed his commission, as the judge, jury, and sheriff, that his name, to the Indians, was associated with unerring retribution for all offenses against the white man. Though they feared, yet they all loved him, for he had a noble nature. He had showed discrimination in his punishments. He was a friend to the defenseless and innocent.

When the Indians met him on this occasion, they talked to him in language something like the following: "O, you great chief! We are glad to see you. We have known you before this day. We have known you in the wars, and you always conquer. You are our father: we are your children; and now whatever you say to us we will do. We are blind. Our heads are like stone. We know but little. We are dark, and need light. Teach us."

In one of Mr. Lee's visits to the States, he brought three of Mr. K'Kay's sons to be educated; and for some time they were members of the Wesleyan Academy, Wilbraham, Mass.

About the time these friends arrived at the mission, a dark, heavy cloud was seen rising in the direction of Mount St. Helens. No special remark was excited by this fact; but, on going to the door the next morning, the missionaries were surprised to see the ground, the trees, the grass,—everything,—sprinkled with ashes. A dark cloud shrouded the sky. It seemed to rain; but the clouds were not dripping water. Something descended gently to the earth, in form like fine sand, —in color, it appeared like ashes. Its odor was that of sulphur. The Indians said it had descended in larger quantities toward Mount St. Helen. Soon the mystery was solved: that mountain had broken forth in a splendid eruption, and the winds had wafted its ashes to the door of the missionaries. Excited by this occurrence, they planned an excursion to the north side of the Columbia River. Here, from a high mountain, near its bank, is one of the sublimest views on the North American Continent. The President's Range, separating middle from lower Oregon, is in full view. Its highest peaks, covered with perpetual snows, resting among the clouds, are named in honor of some of the earlier presidents. The highest is Mount Washington, the next Mount Adams, and so in the order of the presidential administrations.

Amid this group of lofty mountains, Helens threw out its dark cloud of smoke. Its fires seemed smothered, but the issuing volumes of smoke and ashes contrasted impressively with the sparkling snow of the surrounding peaks. Here was great extent of view, and variety of landscape, —the mingling of the beautiful and the sublime. The Oregon River, as it would around the base of the hills, and stretched across the plain, seemed to illustrate the *silent* workings of God's power; while the volcano and the vast range of mountains spoke of its mighty effects.

The missionaries returned to their home, from gazing upon this scene, feeling the force of the lines, —

> "This *awful* God is ours, —
> Our Father and our Friend."

———•———

### WILLIAM M'KENDREE

An Indian lad, who received the above name, lost his parents when he was quite young. From the decease of his parents until he was about twelve years of age, he lived in the family of his uncle. During this time he learned the practices of Indian life. He became expert in spearing salmon, and in catching them in a net. Indeed, he was considered one of the best hunters, of his age, in the Wascapam tribe. From his twelfth year he became a member of the missionary family. He immediately exchanged his Indian dress, which consisted of a poor blanket, for the decent apparel afforded him by his teachers. He showed considerable aptness in working in the garden, and taking care of the cattle of the mission farm. He seemed to be pleased with his new mode of life. He listened, with deep interest, to the stories related to him, by the missionaries, of the States. To his uninstructed mind, what he heard of the great cities and beautiful dwellings of white men, of their mode of traveling, and, most of all, their means of learning and religious instruction, was very wonderful. In his Indian language, he would exclaim, "Wake siar nika nanage Boston ileha," —"It will not be long before I shall see the

United States."

He made considerable progress in learning English, and soon became attentive to religious teaching. During the great revival at the station, he professed to meet with a change of heart; and gave evidence of the truthfulness of his profession by a punctual attendance upon the means of grace, and a consistent life.

Not long after this, Colonel Fremont and his band of explorers stopped at the mission, having been exploring the Rocky Mountains' region. The colonel was now on his way to the Pacific shore, and some of his party having left him, he made a request for a recruit from the neighborhood of the mission. After a consultation with William's teacher, he was engaged to accompany him. William was now about eighteen years of age, active, and somewhat intelligent. His outfit was soon made. A few cows, the reward of his industry, he left with the missionaries. He was supplied with one horse to ride, and another to carry his few articles of bedding, clothes, &c.

Bidding him an affectionate adieu, the missionaries parted with him, after many kind words of counsel concerning his religious habits, and with no little solicitude lest new associates, and an unfavorable business, should injure his piety.

For many months no information was received of William. Fremont and his party had gone to Southern Oregon, and were pressing their adventurous way through its pathless forests. But subsequently an emigrant from the States, who had accompanied Fremont's party, with William, to Southern Oregon, and from thence to the Atlantic States, gave the missionaries the following account.

Fremont took William to Washington, and showed him the wonderful things there to be seen. Thus his long-cherished wish was gratified. He returned with Colonel Fremont to California, was with him during the war in that region, and acquitted himself much to the satisfaction of his employer.

At the close of the war, he married a Spanish woman, and was purposing to return to Oregon. But the most pleasing part of the narrative concerning him was, that he retained his Christian habits. When his companions swore, he would, if he could not dissuade them from the practice, abruptly leave their company. His example was so decided, that some of his associates were influenced to lead a better life. Thus did the seed, sown in prayer, bring forth fruit, even under the most unfavorable circumstances.

———•———

## VISIT TO THE HOT SPRINGS

The missionaries sometimes sought relief from their toil in short excursions into the surrounding country. They endeavored, on these occasions, to unite usefulness with recreation, by obtaining a more full acquaintance with the habits of the Indians; speaking a word of counsel or admonition to those who might never visit the station; and, at the same time, to invigorate their own minds and bodies for renewed exortions in their fields of labor.

Having heard frequent remarks concerning certain "Hot Springs," at a distance of about sixty miles from their residence, they resolved to visit them. They took with them an Indian guide: by his assistance they were led to an encampment, where the natives were gathering a supply of roots for food. One species of these they pound in a mortar, making a kind of pumice; and then, by drying in the sun, make a sweet and nutritious food, which will keep in good condition for months. To this company the missionaries offered the "bread of life." They were received kindly; and, after sowing seed which they prayed might prove fruitful, they proceeded on their journey.

The neighborhood of the Springs, which they soon reached, presented a peculiar appearance. The earth was yellow, seeming to be covered with a sulphureous matter, interspersed with red and blue particles. The rocks were of similar appearance, — all giving evidence that internal fires had, some time, found vent there, and thrown their volcanic flames over the country, to a considerable distance.

Following the Shute's River, which rises in the President's Range of mountains, they soon came upon the Springs. The water, as it gushed forth from the mountain in numerous places, was but little below the boiling point. The Indians declared that their meat, suspended in the streams, as the water bubbled up from the ground, cooked nicely. Whether it would have been considered sufficiently boiled by those who were more accustomed to food well dressed, we do not know. A snake, thrown into the spring, was *skinned* almost instantly!

These springs, seven in number, sent forth a large column of steam, as their waters reached the cold air. After struggling around for a short distance, in separate streams, the waters mingled in a beautiful brook, which settled into a quiet pool. In this our missionaries took a bath, which, from its mild temperature, would have answered for an invalid not able to endure cold water.

Having added to their stock of valuable minerals, with which the place abounded, they returned home, stimulated to renewed labor by this manifestation of God in nature, who can make the solid earth burn as a furnace.

----------●----------

### EQUATOR — HIS TRAGIC END

Equator was the name of an Indian chief. Nature made him a chief. Though not the son of a chief, he was placed at the head of his tribe, the Wascapams, in unanimous acknowledgment of his mental and physical superiority. He seemed born to rule. His person was large and commanding, and his bearing lofty, yet dignified. He moved among his fellow-Indians like one conscious of superiority, never condescending to those little acts of bravado which, whether among savages or civilized men, evidence a mind aspiring after, rather than possessing, true greatness. His head was not flattened, like those of his tribe. He used to say, jocosely, that his parents tried the usual methods of giving it the fashionable shape, but that it was *too hard* to be thus molded. He was therefore known, to some extent, as the "Boston chief," because he had a head like the white men.

When first known at the mission station, he had two wives, after the practice of most of the chiefs. The missionaries tried to show him the wickedness of polygamy, and he finally acknowledged it, and put away one of them, but supported her as before. He had, for a savage, an uncommonly clear perception of what was right; and was, more than was usual, disposed to act honestly. His passions, however, were strong, and, when provoked, he was like the lion disturbed in his retreat by the hunters. But he was not like many of his race, seeking small provocation to anger. His noble nature despised mean conduct; and his eye would flash with the fire of indignation when he saw it in others. He was psssionately fond of his children, and the wife with whom he continued to live. He brought them all to the religious services of the mission, and seemed a willing learner of the great truths of the gospel. Ere long, husband, wife, and adult children, all bowed before God as humble penitents. They severally gave good evidence of a saving change of heart. The wife became ambitious to learn the domestic habits of her female Christian friends, who took much pains to instruct her; while, at the same time, she learned the way of salvation more perfectly. She was amiable and teachable, and won the affections of her teachers. His oldest daughter, Talispam, was taken into the mission family. She gave good evidence that she was born again, but her earthly pilgrimage was short. A rapid consumption brought her to an early grave. Equator mourned with a most bitter mourning; but his grief was not like that of the untaught heathen. Though yet but a babe in Christ, sufficient light rested upon his mind in this hour of affliction to make him, in a good degree, peaceful and submissive.

To Equator the missionaries, when called upon to be absent a short time from the station, committed the care of their families and business. He was faithful in such trusts; but his sense of his dignity as a chief led him to set a high value upon his services. His presence and authority were of great importance in maintaining order in the public religious services. Devout and orderly himself, he allowed no improper behavior by his people.

In 1847, a company of emigrants called at the mission. They charged Equator's people with stealing their horses. This accusation the missionaries believed to be untrue, and Equator indignantly denied it. "What!" said he, with the emphasis of wounded pride and innocence; "am I *a dog*, to steal the Americans' horses?"

But the emigrants imprudently insisted; and, as they retired, they unjustly took the horses of the Indians as pledges for the return of their own. By this act the Indian spirit was fully aroused in the few of the clan who were at home, — the larger number of them having gone to the berry-ground. They demanded of Equator to lead them forth to avenge the insult. It was an hour of trial, — of sore temptation. The enemy of his spiritual good came upon him with his deceptive suggestions: "Must he be a woman, and sit down, and bear such insults? Was he not a brave, — a chief? Had his people not been wronged?" To this the missionaries opposed the teachings of the gospel; but, alas, the fiery spirit of the Indian obtained the mastery of his judgment and he yielded to its sway!

The warriors were armed, and they set forth, and surrounded the emigrants, and commenced taking their horses; but without offering violence to the company. In an evil moment, one of the company leveled his rifle, and gave Equator a mortal wound. For his son to shoot the murderer of his father dead on the spot was the work of a moment. A general skirmish now commenced, in which several on both sides were wounded, and the whites fled toward the Willamette Valley.

Equator, leaning upon the arm of the missionary, who had been an eye-witness of the scene, was led into the mission house. He bled profusely, and was in great agony. It was evident that his end was nigh. He expressed great regret that he had not listened to his faithful teachers; and, it was hoped, sincerely repented of this, the only act discreditable to his profession he had been known to commit. May we not hope that He who saved the dying thief accepted him at the last?

————•————

## A BRAND PLUCKED FROM THE BURNING

In the fall of 1846, Colonel Fremont called at the Dalles mission. He had been, with his company, surveying among the Rocky Mountains during the summer; and, being short of provision, had pitched his camp near the mission, that his men might remain there, while he, with a few attendants, should go to Vancouver, to procure a fresh supply. After his return, and when they were about to start for the States, one of his party deserted, and came to the mission house. He was an ill-clothed and fierce-looking man. He declared, at once, that he was determined not to return with Fremont. "Let him shoot me," said he, in an angry tone; "I will not return with him." A blood-thirsty spirit seemed to possess him. "I will kill Fremont," he exclaimed, "if he comes here: I will fell him to the floor!"

Just at this point of time Fremont was seen coming toward the mission house.

Mr. C________, the deserter, repeated his threat of encountering him. He had no weapon but a long knife. The resolution of Fremont, and the decision with which he acted, was well known to the missionaries; they could not doubt the fatal consequences to the deserter, if the attempt was made. Besides, they wished not to see, if they could possibly prevent it, a deadly encounter in their house, dedicated to "peace and good will to all men." They earnestly entreated C________ to retire in an opposite direction from that of the approach of Colonel Fremont. The entreaties of the *wife* finally prevailed, and he sullenly retired into a back yard, muttering that he should meet him as he returned.

The colonel entered, to bid the missionaries a courteous adieu, as he was about to leave for the States. In the course of conversation, he alluded to one Mr. C________, who had deserted, saying he was a reckless and dangerous man, and that it would be his painful duty to hang him, if he was retaken.

After he had left, Mr. C________ re-entered at the opposite door. He had been, he said, standing near the barn, by which one path to the camp led. "If," said he, "Colonel Fremont had come *that* way, I should have attacked him." Doubtless, the failure of meeting with his brave enemy was not altogether unwelcome to this boasting desperado; and it was certainly a mercy to himself, whether he had been the victim or the murderer, that the conflict did not take place.

It was in nowise agreeable to the missionaries to have such a man under their roof; but it was now too late in the season for the usual communication with the Willamette, and they consented that he might spend the winter with them, on his giving assurance of good conduct.

Fremont and his party having gone, and the hardened man having become somewhat softened by kind treatment, he gave to the missionaries the following brief account of his life: —

"I was," said he, "educated by pious parents. My father was a Methodist local preacher, and I have a brother in the Methodist ministry. From a boy, I have been wicked. I ran away, when young, from my parental home; and, step by step, I have plunged into the greatest sins. I have been a gambler, a thief, a burglar, an extensive counterfeiter. There remained only one more outrageous act to complete the catalogue of my crimes, and that was *murder*, which, but for you, I might have committed.

"I am now free from my associates, by whom I have been helped to sin, though one of the most wicked among them. The wages of sin, with me, have been hard. I am now determined to live a *moral life*; to be honest and useful. I cannot — I do not — expect to be a *Christian*: that would be to expect too much, — my sins are too black. I am *sure*," he added, with bitterness, "that I am *lost*, — lost forever! If I were in hell, I could not be more certain."

Of this conviction the missionaries tried to relieve his mind. They pointed him to the sufficiency of the atonement for all the truly penitent. But he persisted in his unfavorable view of his eternal prospects, and made no efforts to become a Christian. He, however, attended the meetings, and frequently listened to personal efforts for his conversion. Thus time passed off somewhat pleasantly until February. He had been about four months at the mission, making himself useful in various ways, as a mechanic.

At this time he had an altercation with some Indians who visited the premises, and threatened to proceed to violent measures against them. This course was likely to create much trouble, and to disturb the good feelings of the Indians toward the missionaries themselves. They therefore insisted upon his leaving. This he did, with much ill will, threatening to destroy the mission.

During the following summer nothing was heard of this desperate man. But in the fall, at a camp-meeting, in the Willamette Valley, he made his appearance. As the meeting progressed, the Spirit wrought powerfully upon him. As he expressed it, "The Spirit seemed to say, 'This once I strive; *now* be saved, or never.' " He threw himself into the circle of prayer in great agony. His self-reproaches were very bitter. He literally tore up the earth where he knelt, in his convulsive struggles. All night did he pray, with tears; and all night the people of God kneeled around him, in earnest supplication. At the dawn of day, light from above burst in upon his mind. He soon became filled with heavenly peace. It was truly a life from the dead, — the light of day flashing in upon midnight darkness! He afterward related his experience, with great simplicity, and all were much affected.

He remained at the mission in Willamette, from this time, about three months; showing the genuineness of his conversion by a holy life. He then left, for his long-forsaken home in the States, where he is now married, and, it is believe, is still continuing to lead a new life, in Christ.

———————•———————

## NOTES OF A JOURNEY

The difficulties and dangers of traveling in Oregon, during the residence of our missionaries, were very great. If the journey was by land or water, or partly, as was generally the case, by both, the perils and labor were much the same.

In the month of September several of the mission family started from the Dalles for the Willamette Valley, a distance of one hundred and fifty miles. The first difficulty was to hire Indian assistance. This was not a small matter, for they are not easily satisfied with the first engagement, and are often still more difficult to be satisfied in the final settlement. Next, the canoes were put in readiness; then the food for the whole company was carefully provided, with some little conveniences with which to prepare it for eating. Besides these, a small quantity of wheat was carefully stowed away, to be ground at Willamette.

All the *temporal* preparations being made, the company were called together for devotional exercises. A hymn was sung, in which the sons of the forest were ever interested. Then, in turn, the Christian teachers invoked the blessing of God to attend them, — to preserve them from the perils of the waters, and the perils of the wilderness, — from the dangers of exposure to drenching rains and chilling winds. Most of all, they prayed that they might behold the face of their Christian friends at the Willamette in peace, and return renewed in spiritual and bodily vigor for the great work of winning the heathen to Christ. Having thus sought the divine protection, they bade adieu, with no little emotion, to the native converts, who accompanied them to their boats.

The voyage down the Columbia to the Cascades occupied a little over two days. At night, a camp was formed on shore; a cheerful fire rendered their resting place comfortable, while its light, reflected from the surrounding forest, rendered its darkness more gloomy. But, while the howl of savage beasts was occasionally mingled with the shout of savage men, a sound stranger in this wilderness was heard. It was the sound of prayer and praise, sent forth from our little band, to awake the echoes of the forest.

The Cascades, formed by a narrow opening for the Columbia, through the President's Range of mountains, with its rocky beds, and lofty, jagged, overhanging precipices, exhibit one of the wildest scenes in nature.

The portage round these rapids being attended with much delay and labor, our travelers decided to trust to their frail canoe. The danger to which they were exposed heightened the intense emotion excited by the terrific scenery, and profound silence reigned among the voyagers, except when broken by the involuntary "Thank God," as some perilous point was passed in safety; or, by the wild shout of the Indians, as they successfully cleared a projecting rock, against which they seemed about to be dashed.*

Thus for two miles, sometimes in a smooth but rapid current, at other moments tossed upon waves white with foam, the kind providence of God guided them safely; and soon they were sailing pleasantly toward Vancouver, twenty miles distant.

Just below the Cascades, they encamped upon a peninsula, slightly connected, by a barren strip of land, with the main shore. They soon perceived that their position, thus separated from the surrounding country, was most providential. The whole forest, for many miles, was one glowing, terrific sheet of flame. The neighboring mountain peaks, four thousand feet high, burned with fearful intensity. The night was dark, save the lurid glare of this ocean of fire. The

*  See Frontispiece.

roaring of the flames, the crash of falling trees, and the fierce, despairing shriek of the wild animals, constituted one of the most awfully sublime scenes ever witnessed. Truly, these are a *part* of *thy* ways, O God! In the tempest, the flood, and conflagration, *thou* art seen! How insignificant is man compared with thee!—

> "Yes! as a drop of water in the sea,
> *All this magnificence in Thee is lost*:
> What are ten thousand worlds compared to thee?
> And what am *I*, then? Heaven's unnumber'd host,
> Though multiplied by myriads, and array'd
> In all the glory of sublimest thought,
> Is but an atom in the balance:—weigh'd
> Against *thy* greatness, is a cipher brought
> Against Infinity!" *   *   *   *   *

In the morning, the missionaries gathered their company together, for early devotions, in preparation for their continued voyage. The intense emotions experienced during the night had prevented sleep; and now *God* seemed unusually near. A suffocating smoke pervaded the whole atmosphere, and rendered their progress slow and difficult. At night, having made but little progress, they encamped within two miles of Vancouver.

The following day being the Sabbath, a little band of natives of the vicinity were added to the company; and the word of life was offered, from the text: "Almost thou persuadest me to be a Christian." Though *nature's temple* was their place of worship, yet God, "who dwellest not in temples made with hands," came into the midst of his people,—their hearts were elevated to him, and they felt a new preparation for their responsible work. Without any other special incident, they reached the settlement at Willamette. Here they spent a few days in the pleasant associations of Christian friendship. To those surrounded by the heathen, the value of the society of those whose minds have been enlightened by the gospel, and hose hearts have been renewed by divine grace, is unspeakably great.

On the return voyage, a short stay was made at Vancouver, for supplies, with which a canoe was filled. While passing along the banks, still smoking with the recent fire, a large bear came limping along, scorched and bleeding, and, no doubt, homeless. Some of the Indians, true to their unpitying nature, seized a tomahawk and rifle, to make him their prize; but he plunged in among the ruins, and eluded their pursuit. They returned, exclaiming, "He is badly off." Bruin loved life, and preferred an uncomfortable refuge, with bleeding and pain, to death from the tomahawk or rifle.

Not far from this place, one of the Indians, while wandering some distance from the company in the canoe, discovered a retired hut, in which a white man, his wife, and two children had made their forest home. The father and husband lay dead, and the afflicted partner and little ones, with none near to sympathize, to counsel, or to assist. How timely must have been the approach of those who could not only relieve the pressure of outward necessity, but point the widow and the orphans to their God and Comforter!

While this illustration of the exposure of the emigrant in this new country was deeply impressing their minds, a still more sad illustration occurred of the surrounding moral darkness. Near the bank of the Columbia river, in a retired nook, without any covering, without a burial, lay the corpse of a Shasta slave, — a girl of about sixteen years of age. The truth soon flashed upon the minds of the missionaries. Surrounding circumstances, and the known practice of the Indians, established in their minds the fact, that this poor girl, away from her tribe and friends, while sick, and perhaps helpless, was brought here to die! All that our missionaries could now do, they did. They gave her a decent burial, while they dropped a tear over the sad condition of those who sit in the region and shadow of death.

While dispirited by these sad events, a messenger overtook the company, with letters from the States. It was like the breaking of morning upon a night of darkness and danger. One of their number thus notes, in substance, the incident: "A letter from *my mother* always begets deep emotion; but, under such circumstances, it was overwhelming. I had thrown myself down, while a deep gloom seemed pervading my mind. I started when the messenger came, and the next moment I seemed to be *at home*, conversing with my dear parent." Thus does the providence of God most wisely mingle joy with sorrow, and kindly interpose when our burden becomes oppresive.

After about twenty days' absence, our friends again reached their mission station, with a lively sense of God's preserving care and abundant goodness, and resolved, with new consecration, to give themselves to his work.

———•———

## MARY AND MARIA

The fathers of Mary and Maria were Englishmen. In their early days they had left their island home, entered the employment of the Hudson's Bay Company, and engaged in hunting the buffalo and stag, and trapping the beaver, in the Red River country of Canada. They married wives of the Kree tribe of Indians, and each had a numerous family. The neighborhood of their settlement had become somewhat populous, from the large number of men, from the Company's service, who settled there.

These adventurous men began to wish for another field in which to gratify their love of new scenes and boundless forests. At this time the fame of Oregon reached them. They determined at once to start for that far-off country. Early in the spring of 1841 they commenced their weary pilgrimage. At first they carried their goods and children in horse-carts. Soon they abandoned these because of the roughness of the way, and placed their beds, provisions, and indispensable articles on pack-saddles. The hardy women and children followed the train on foot, with an occasional relief on the back of heavily-loaded horses. Thus they spent, on the way, the entire summer.

In October the tired but not dispirited travelers arrived at the mission station. Here they received sympathy, and what aid the circumstances afforded, together with passing words of religious instruction. The children were much exhausted, and it was yet a long journey to the Willamette Valley, their place of destination. The parents, therefore, proposed to leave their two interesting girls, Mary and Maria, in the mission families. Mary was eight and Maria eleven years of age. We are enabled to speak more particularly of Mary. She had never learned to read, consequently the missionaries commenced teaching her the alphabet. Her progress was slow, at first. She manifested but little interest in her lessons, until, one day, as she was listlessly repeating what she was being taught, a new thought suddenly entered her mind. Looking up into her teacher's face, she inquired, "Does all reading mean something?" "Certainly," was the reply. From that moment, says her instructor, the scales seemed to fall from her eyes; and, with great rapidity and never failing interest, she progressed in her education. Her kind friends now received much pleasure in teaching her; and in ten months, the time of her stay with them, she had become able to read with tolerable correctness.

Maria was a more active and thoughtful child than Mary. She, too, learned to read. Both received religious instruction in the family, and in the Sabbath school, at which they were constant attendants. While they were learning that they must "be born again," and that Christ died "to save sinners," the Spirit of God was evidently graciously impressing the truth upon their hearts. Frequently would Maria call for Mary, and request permission for them to retire to some secret place for prayer; for the same privilege Mary would often seek Maria's company.

At the end of ten months the father of Mary came, to conduct them both to their friends, in the Willamette settlement. They requested to meet their teachers once more for religious instruction. The father witnessed, with apparent interest, their proficiency in reading and knowledge, as they were examined by their teachers. After the exercises were closed, they both appeared sad. Maria gave frank expression to her feelings: "If we do not get new hearts now," said she, "I fear we never shall."

"Are you ready *now*," asked their teachers, "to give your hearts of stone to Christ, and receive tender and believing hearts?" They both expressed a wish to make the effort. All bowed together at the footstool of mercy; and, in answer to prayer, God manifested his renewing Spirit. Joy and gladness filled the souls of these little lambs, and, with their teachers, they shouted aloud the praises of a sin-forgiving Saviour. The Christian friends, including several native converts, of the neighborhood, heard the sound of their rejoicing, and came in to be partakers of their joy.

Thus clearly and most providentially were these little wanderers in the wilderness prepared to return to their paternal roof. Mary's father was seriously impressed with what he saw, but did not obtain pardon of his sins.

The next day these children left the house of their religious instructors, receiving many earnest and prayerful entreaties to "hold fast whereunto they had attained." From that time we have learned nothing of Mary and Maria. But we confidently hope that the seed scattered in tears, which had so promisingly taken root, will bear sheaves, to be gathered at last into the garner of God.

---

## SCIATS

While we have presented sketches of some Indians upon whom the gospel seemed to have a decided influence, making them new creatures in Christ, it may be both interesting and profitable to exhibit the traits of character in a few who remained unchanged.

The missionary to the Indian is called to endure the provocations of such dayly. He must show them that the servant of God must not strive, but be gentle toward all men. The untamed savage will not always appreciate the meekness of love, but the incidents in the closing portion of this sketch will show that ferocity will quail before Christian calmness. At the same time we may learn the dangers of personal violence, to which they are often subjected who have counted not their lives dear unto them, that they might preach Jesus, and him crucified, to those who know not God, and are without hope in the world.

Sciats was accounted a chief among his people. He was boastful and forward in his intercourse with the missionaries. Though he did not very frequently beg, yet when he *requested*, it was intended to have the force of a command, for, said he, "*I am a chief.*"

Sciats attained to an office, which, though not without its influence for good upon others perhaps, did not soften the spirit nor correct the manners of its possessor. The Indian agent had made him whipper-in-chief. Sciats became, under this appointment, more a terror than ever to his red brethren. He would come to the mission house, and, in a self-congratulating tone, say, "Well, friend, I have killed two this morning."

"Killed two!" was the reply; "did you *kill* them?"

"Why, in *our way of speaking*, I did. I whipped them, as this whip can tell," flourishing at the same time a riding-whip, "I whipped them until they lay on the ground as dead men."

Having become of increased importance, in his own eyes, Sciats thought to add some slaves to his attendants. He appeared at the mission house, one morning, dressed for an important mission. A profusion of feathers decorated his hair. All the ornaments of his scanty wardrobe were carefully displayed. He was going to the Klamath tribe, to purchase two slaves, in exchange for two horses. The distance was about ten days' ride, and Sciats felt that he was on an important and great mission.

The missionary remonstrated with him upon the wickedness of his projected business; telling him that a "chief" and a "master-whipper" ought to set a better example.

At this Sciats's dignity was offended. Throwing down his whip and rope, he exclaimed, in great anger, "Your talk is not good: I will whip you;" and commenced at once to tie the feet of the Christian teacher. But soon relenting, he took his whip and rope, mounted his horse, and off he rode to the Klamaths, for his slaves. He returned with two; but they soon ran away, and Sciats found that this species of ungodliness, at least, was not gain. He never recovered the fugitives.

Soon after the above incidents, the agent visited the mission station, and, learning the bad conduct of Sciats, ordered him to receive the punishment which he had so joyfully inflicted upon others. The Indians exulted at the sentence; but decided that as there was no chief greater than Sciats but the agent himself, he must inflict the punishment. As the Indians say they do not believe in whipping *clothes*, his back, according to custom, was laid bare, and twenty-five lashes laid on by the "great chief." Sciats, true to his former profession, insisted that the whipping was good, and that he should be a better man.

Sciats had not been without his pretensions to piety; sometimes saying to the missionaries, "Friends, I pray in my family. I don't forget to pray in secret." His whipping even he seemed determined to turn to the account of his godliness. The next Sabbath he came to the mission house, with his Testament, requesting the leaves turned down at the places where it said Paul was whipped. They were found, and read to him; and he turned away, muttering, with great complaisance, "Ah, Paul was whipped! Paul was a good man. Sciats, he was whipped."

The agent had encouraged the Indians to cultivate the land. The missionaries also labored constantly to secure in them an interest in farming, but with too little success. They plowed their land, gave them seed, directed them in the proper method of cultivation, and assisted them in building log-houses, in the vicinity of their fields.

Sciats gave some attention to this business; and, being a chief, he claimed more assistance than others. He had, at one time, a fine field of wheat, corn, and potatoes. Again and again he was urged to inclose it, or build his log-house near, and watch it. He was warned of the consequences of a neglect of this, where the cattle were allowed to feed at large, and no responsibility was assumed by their owners for any damage they might do to uninclosed and unwatched crops. But his idleness was greater than his fear of loss. When his crops were nearly ready for harvesting, one night, the cattle of his missionary friend destroyed the whole. He hurried to the station, burning with rage and disappointment. "Your cattle," said he, "have *eat all*; left nothing, — no, nothing!" He demanded immediate reparation. The acknowledgment of such a demand, under such circumstances, was contrary to all example, and would have involved the missionaries in an insupportable taxation, to pay for their neighbors' neglect of a required protection for their fields.

Sciats came repeatedly, urging more and more violently his claim. He was reasoned with, put off, and finally flatly refused. His anger was furious. He stamped and threatened. Casting his eye around for something with which to wreak his vengeance, a clock met his gaze. The loss of this, and this he seemed determined to dash to the floor; but his Christian teacher took him calmly by the arm, and led him from the house, toward the residence of a neighboring missionary. Just after reaching the house, his anger began to burn again. "Have I no gun at my house?" he exclaimed, and dashed away to his hut, a short distance off, furious as a bear robbed of her whelps. What was to be done? He would probably be back in a few moments, armed with a loaded gun. The missionary had a two-barreled gun behind his door: "There," said he, "it shall stay, unloaded. I will trust in God, and bide the consequence." He entered his dwelling, and sat down calmly, to wait the approach of his enemy. Friendly Indians gathered around, and extended their sympathy; but no Sciats came. The night passed away.

Early in the morning, Sciats came, through a circuituous rout, to the mission station. He called at the neighbor of the injured missionary, confessing his fault, and begging him to go and intercede for him. He led Sciats to his injured friend.

"I no sleep," said he, "all night, — I feel so bad, — I use you so bad;" and, with evident brokenness of spirit, he craved forgiveness.

He was, of course, forgiven, and directed to Him who alone can blot out the sinner's transgressions.

From that time Sciats remained an undeviating friend to the missionaries. His haughty bearing yielded to the power of a gentle firmness, united with love. Could the sword of the soldier have done more? Was this warlike savage insensible to the influence of superior goodness? Though we find no record of Sciats's hopeful conversion, deep indeed must have been the religious impressions which could draw from "a chief" such confessions of wrong doing!

## TILUSTINA

We have introduced into these "incidents" several narratives of heathen children. We desire our young readers, who have been blessed with a Christian education, to be able to contrast their situation with that of the boys and girls whose parents are in the darkness of heathenism. We wish also to portray to them the happy effects of Bible instruction upon these childrens' minds. We hope, by so doing, to render more cheerful the contributions of our readers to the missionary cause, and to induce them to make still greater sacrifices to help the extension of the gospel "into all the world."

Some time in the winter or spring of 1842 a little Indian girl might have been seen standing at the door of the missionary house, asking admittance. She was almost without apparel. Her body was covered with filth and vermin. She begged to be admitted into the family, to assist in the household duties. Though repulsive in her appearance, and although it must necessarily be some time before she could be of any service in the family, she was kindly received. A thorough ablution, and clean and decent, though coarse, clothes, soon made her person more agreeable.

In a few months she became quite serviceable, being able to assist in washing, attending the table-work, and taking care of the babe. She also made some progress in reading and writing. Before the close of the year she began to appreciate the contrast between her situation and her former poverty. She would congratulate herself in reference to the happy change: "Then," she would say, "I had no clothes,—only one poor piece of baize; now I have one, two dresses, a handkerchief, and a blanket. Then I lived in a miserable wigwam,—my bed a mat, with a piece of skin for a covering; now I have a comfortable home. Then I was often hungry and without food; now I have enough to eat. Call me a 'Boston,' " she would say; "for I am just like a 'Boston.' "

Her Indian mates envied and sometimes perplexed her. They would tease her to beg for them, of the mission family, things which she knew it was improper for them to have. She seldom asked for favors, except for food to carry to her mother, which was occasionally granted her.

At the camp-meeting, of which an account has been given, Telustina professed to partake of the rich mercy of God, in the pardon of her sins. Though young, and possessed of a limited knowledge of religious truth, in comparison with the children of our highly-favored Sabbath schools, and though she had her faults, yet she gave good evidence that her heart had been renewed. She attended the means of grace, and seemed to be faithful to her private devotions. At the family altar she sometimes became exceedingly happy, and, rejoicing in the Lord, would cry out, "O Jesus, thou art good! My heart rejoices in thee! I am happy,—I am happy!"

After she had been with the mission family for a considerable time, she thought she understood all kinds of "Boston work," and could do it properly and expeditiously. It was thought best, therefore, for her to take care of herself. She had intimated her purpose of marrying no one but one of "the Boston men;" having, as she thought, so much knowledge of their method of housekeeping, and feeling so much sympathy with them. She, however, became the wife of a "King George's man," a name by which all the English are designated by the Indians.

She and her husband settled in the Willamette Valley, where he had the charge of a mill. The missionaries visited her and her family once, some time after her marriage. They found them in a romantic situation. A stream rushed over its rocky bed, near their door. Their furniture was simple, but she appeared happy in the religion which her visitors had previously taught her, having, also, a kind husband. She showed her affectionate remembrance of them by giving her first child the name of theirs.

How different her situation from that of her heathen countrywomen! How quiet, but powerful, were the influences of the gospel upon Tilustina! How different her home, surrounded by the unostentatious but really important conveniences of civilization, from the filthy wigwam, the cheerless residence in which she spent her early youth! Truly, the ways of religion are pleasantness, and her followers have the promise of blessings in this world, as well as glory hereafter.

------•------

### KIS-KIS, OR THE FOOLISH END

The missionaries regarded Kis-kis as in no wise a superior man; but in his own nation he was called "a brave." He was reckless in his adventures, headstrong, and without wisdom. He boasted that he had no fear; but he showed that he was too stupid to discern danger. He could throw his brawny arms into the air and raise the wild shout of the warrior, when there was no provocation to fight and rush to battle without even the low motives of a savage.

Kis-kis had a congenial friend in Skakaps, a neighbor. This Kis-kis was the father of Tilustina, of whom we have given an account; and it was when he came to leave his daughter with the missionaries that they first became acquainted with him.

Kis-kis and Skakaps started off, one day, for the Klamath tribe, to trade in beaver skins. Having lost their way, they arrived among the Klamaths weary and dispirited.

"You have come in a good time, brothers," said a Klamath.

"To get food, and rest, and trade?" replied the visitors.

"And to fight for us too," replied the Klamath chief.

At this proposal Kis-kis feigned an indifference he did not feel; for he desire more blankets and guns, though he seemed to love fighting for its own sake.

"Braves don't fight for nothing," said Kis-kis.

"I will give you my daughter, to be your wife."

"Too many wives," answered Kis-kis, who already had two.

"More wives, more salmon," replied the chief.

Whether this consideration moved Kis-kis or not we cannot tell, but he closed in with the offer, and agreed to fight, assisted only by his companion, the enemies of the Klamaths. It appeared that the Klamaths had just returned from an excursion against the Shastas, and were beaten in battle; and a brother of the chief had been killed.

"Take revenge for my brother," said the chief to Kis-kis. "You live with the pale-faces. You know much. We know nothing. The Klamaths and the Shastas fight, as their fathers fought, with bows. Go, — bring us the scalps of our enemies. You are brave.

Thus did the wily chief flatter the vain-glorious warrior to his ruin. After a long and fatiguing journey, Kis-kis and Skakaps, with a Klamath guide, came in sight of the Shastas' lodges. The sun was sinking behind the hills. Their enemies, who had never provoked *them*, were sauntering carelessly about the encampment, suspecting no danger. Suddenly, our adventurers opened their fire. The women, unused to fire-arms, were frantic with fear. The old warriors seized their bows, and sprang for the trees. For some time the guns seemed more than equal to the superior number of bows; but soon the unskillful firing of Kis-kis became evident to his enemies, and they became more bold. They pressed hard upon him from every side. A poisoned arrow at length pierced his thigh: he stumbled, and his friends fled with desperate haste. Poor Kis-kis fought with the courage of despair, but soon fell dead, pierced with many arrows.

The missionaries tried to use all these sad occurrences to impress on the minds of the heathen the superior excellence of the gospel of peace. In many cases, we trust, the seed fell upon good ground.

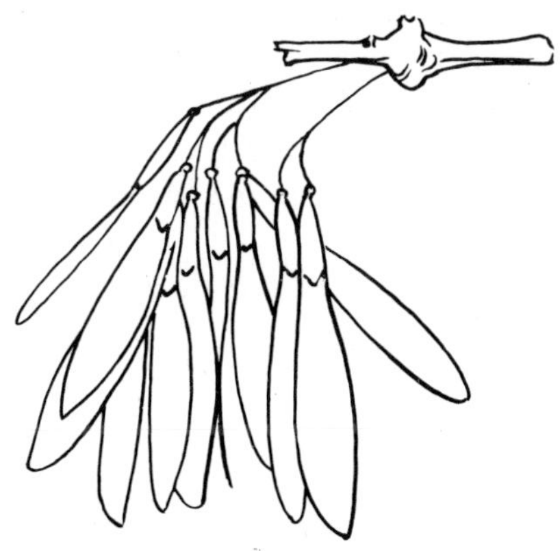

# VISIT TO MOUNT JOHN ADAMS

## EXTRACTS FROM A JOURNAL

*Dalles Mission Station, Oregon Territory, September 13, 1845.* —Great preparation must be made in this country for a journey, either by water or land. We have just completed our arrangements for an excursion to Mount Adams. Provisions for three persons for ten days, tents, &c., with pack-horses to carry the same, make, in part, our outfit. The two boys who have assisted me upon the farm, Penassar and Howatt, accompany me.

Mount John Adams is the only one of the President's Range to be seen from the mission house. Its ever snow-clad summit is a beautiful object, as it reposes amid the clouds. In a direct line, it may be fifty miles from this station, though our track along the Indian trail will be perhaps a hundred miles.

*In camp, at night.* —We have made about thirty miles to-day. We swam our horses across the Columbia, and were taken over ourselves in a canoe by the Indians. Our camp is at the foot of a large mountain. I am much fatigued, but shall rest to-morrow from secular labor, and endeavor to refresh both soul and body in the service of God.

*14th, Sabbath Morning.* —The quiet that reigns through this forest is favorable to the spirit of devotion, —God is here. While I think of Christian lands, —of my own favored countrymen, —of my dear friends, with whom I have walked to the house of God in company, —I am thankful that I can here, in this solitary place, commune with my Maker. After our morning devotions, my heart was greatly strengthened in endeavoring to instruct my Indian boys in a knowledge of the Bible. Could the Sabbath-school children of the States see them, as their countenances occasionally are lighted up, when they receive a few rays of gospel truth, they would more than ever love the missionary cause.

*15th.* —We commenced our journey this morning before the day broke, and have threaded our way along the sides of lofty mountain peaks, across streams, and through almost impassable forests, until, having traveled thirty miles, we have pitched our tents on the "Indian Berry Ground." Here are a large company of Indians, busily engaged in picking whortleberries: these they dry by the fire, and preserve them for future use. They spend a month or more here, every season.

The absence of our Indian converts so long a time during the berry season, being surrounded as they are by every possible bad example, and separated from the watchful care of their teachers, in many cases proves very injurious to their piety. We mourn over their frequent declensions, and feel keenly the difficulties of our work; but God is our help.

This evening I held a meeting with the Indians, and gave them such counsel as their circumstances seemed to require.

*16th.*—We rose early this morning, and held a meeting with the Indians. Though the day had only begun to dawn, a good number were present to hear of Christ crucified, and to join in an early song of praise.

It was our intention to ascend Mount Adams, which is just before us, and return to this place to-night. We left our tent and provision on the Berry Ground, in charge of the boys, and, with a guide, started to ascend the mountain.

We reached the foot about eleven o'clock, A.M., after having traveled about twelve miles from our camp; though, when we started, we seemed to be within a few miles of it. My guide, an old man, of the Tlikatal tribe, said I was the first white man who had tried to climb to the summit. As we slowly wended our way up the side of the mountain, the scene became overwhelmingly beautiful and grand! From the foot to the region of snow is a growth of heavy timber, of fir, spruce, &c. Just before entering upon the domains of perpetual winter, the evidences of terrific avalanches became apparent,—deep excavations in the earth, fragments of scattered rocks, and tottering crags, left trembling upon their base by the mighty shock which had made such devastation,—all showed how fearfully grand must have been the course of the avalanche, from this far height to the plain below!

Arriving at the region of snow, we left our horses, and commenced climbing as best we could, the old man leading, and my young guide and myself following. Having ascended a considerable distance from the horses, the old man stopped, exhausted. "See," said he, putting his fingers into his gray locks, which were tossing in the wind, "I am old,—old limbs weary. Go; you are young. By and by you too get old,—then weary soon." So saying, he rested awhile, gave us a few words of direction, and returned to the horses.

With determined minds we climbed up,—up,—picking our way along the ridges, where there was no snow. The moss-flower, scattered here and there, was in full bloom. Tracks of deer were sometimes to be seen, and the elk frequently crossed our path. Having, with much labor, ascended to within one thousand feet, perhaps, of the top, I sat down, exhausted, and determined to go no further. The sun was fast sinking in the distant west, and the country below glowed in his reflected rays. My soul was absorbed in the sublimity of the scene. Just below us were yawning chasms, whose fearful depths the eye of man never pierced Stretched out on every side, in the mingling of earth and sky, were forests, mountains, plains, and rivers, all wild, and grand as ever human eye beheld.

"These are *thy* works, Parents of good."

The hills of Willamette, one hundred and fifty miles, and the Columbia River, at Vancouver, one hundred miles distant, were distinctly seen by the unaided eye.

The approaching evening, and the increasing chilliness of the air, broke a reverie which I would have delighted to indulge for hours, and we commenced our return. Every step seemed a plunge, so sharp was the descent, and so sensitive was my exhausted frame.

About ten o'clock we reached the horses. The old man had left for his lodge, six miles distant, requesting us to follow him, for a night's repose. But I could go no further. Buttoning up my coat, I laid down on the cold, hard ground, and passed a restless night.

In the morning, having just started, we met the old guide, coming to meet us, having a few berries. These, and more that were given us soon after, by some Dalles Indians, were very acceptable after fasting, with the exception of a very few berries, for thirty hours. We found our tents and friends all safe, on our arrival at the Berry Ground. Here I held meetings again with the Indians. Experience has taught us, that the only way to secure a permanent influence over these wanderers of the forest, is to follow them in their journeyings, so far as possible; holding meetings with them, and watching over their spiritual welfare.

*20th.* — We reached our home to-day, having had an instructive and, we hope, not a profitless excursion.

## LUXILLU

Luxillu was a native of Wisham, a village at the Dalles, on the north side of the Columbia River. His native language was the Walla-walla. As it is quite common for the different tribes to intermarry, he obtained a wife from the Chenocks. Luxillu and Wapaspa, his wife, lived happily together. Their children all died in infancy.

During the great revival of 1838, Luxillu and his wife experienced the pardoning grace of God, as did a large number of the Indians, both young and old. Luxillu was one of the faithful few who continued in undeviating fidelity to his profession. In his lodge he was mild and devotional, faithfully attending to his social duties as a Christian. The family altar was never without the sacrifice of prayer and praise. In the stated prayer-meetings, Luxillu's voice of confession of Christ was seldom wanting; and his devotional spirit fully evinced his sincerity.

John, of whom an account is given in a following section, was his intimate friend. They built log-houses together, toiled in the canoe side by side, and could almost always be seen in each other's company. They were kindred spirits, helping each other in the way to heaven.

Luxillu was an excellent interpreter. He seemed to catch, as the missionaries never knew any other Indian to do, the *spirit* of the language communicated to him. When he was absent during the fishing or berry season, away from the stated means of grace, and surrounded with temptations, he stood firm. He always returned rejoicing in the love of God. As might be expected, confidence in his piety was inspired in the minds of his companions, though they were unconverted. His influence for good was extensive. It affected all who knew his spirit and life.

When his teachers left the Dalles for the Willamette Valley, in anticipation of returning to their own country, he accompanied them with a heavy heart. He had loved them for their works' sake, and he loved *them* because he loved *Him* who had sent them to tell him of the cross of Christ. When, at last, the time came for them to embark for the States, this faithful disciple, like the companions of Paul, accompanied them to the beach, and bade them farewell with many prayers and tears, sorrowing, as did the apostle's friends, because he thought to see their faces no more.

Luxillu was an ornament to his Christian profession, and a bright light amid the darkness of heathenism.

————•————

## JOHN

John was introduced to the mission family by his chief, Tumeocool. Tumeocool spoke warmly in his praise, — said he was active, and would be of great help on the farm. This was found to be true. He brought his wife and father, Simeon, of whom we have written. After some time, he built a log-hut for his family, and cast off his Indian dress, and obtained by his industry, for the Sabbath, a full suit of clothes, like the "Bostons." With these he was much pleased. He even, at first, showed the weakness — at which we can hardly be surprised in *him* — of affecting the fop. He had seen the vain young Americans, at the Willamette, make a show of their white handkerchiefs, and he was careful to let his hang slily from his pocket. But John was a rare specimen of the natives of the forest. Like Luxillu, his friend, he was apt to learn. He was very ambitious to do things as the "Bostons" did them, and as well as they. He drove the team, labored with much tact in the saw-pit, helped to get out lumber, (a most toilsome business,) and even showed, some mechanical skill. He was, too, an apt interpreter. When most of the congregation were Chenooks, and the teacher spoke in their language, John would interpret, with great sobriety, into Walla-walla, for those of that people who were present.

He had two children, for whom he sought "Boston" names. Herbert and Julia were his much-loved son and daughter, in whose improvement in civilization and Christian instruction he took great delight. We are not informed concerning the circumstances of John's conversion, but he was one of the few native Christians in whom the missionaries took unabated delight. He was always at his class and prayer meeting, and delighted greatly in the preached word, and in the Lord's supper. John's piety was uniform. In revivals and declensions, at the mission, and on the hunting or fishing ground, his zeal failed not. He labored too, from lodge to lodge, to bring sinners to Christ. On a few occasions, he was sent out to conduct religious service with his countrymen; and in this service his labors were greatly blessed.

Such was another instance of the fruit of missionary labor. Is not one-such soul won to Christ worth a life of toil? Who will say, though many are the discouragements of the missionary, that he labors in vain, and spends his strength for naught? Christ will delight, we doubt not, to own such as Luxillu and John as his jewels, in the day of his coming.

———•———

## KLADAKULA

Kladakula was a Chenook chief, and a medicine man. He was tall and stout, possessing a muscular frame of great strength. His hard, almost fiendish countenance, proud step, and air of defiance, made him altogether one of the most intimidating savages of the country. He lived, with a small clan of his people, about ten miles below the Dalles mission. His introduction to the missionary of that station was not the most propitious. He was detected stealing from his wheat field. Taking some friendly Indians, the missionary went out, and remonstrated with him. He responded to the kind entreaty by taking his pistol from his belt, and coolly priming it; intimating, at the same time, that he should take wheat when he wanted it, and as much as he liked.

Not long afterward this undesirable neighbor took up his residence in the vicinity of the mission. He was disposed to be altogether too intimate; trying, in the true Indian style, to beg whatever he fancied and thought was in the possession of the mission. It was soon found that, where giving would not satisfy, withholding was the true policy; and he met, at all times, with a mild but firm refusal. Thus matters stood for awhile, when Kladakula seems to have made up his mind to try the patience of these Christian white men, and to see if by threats and savage bearing he could not obtain his objects. Coming in, one day, with a sullen countenance and lowering brow, he sat awhile in threatening silence. He then began to complain that *his* people never got presents from the mission, and that other Indians were more highly favored. As this was not true, it was firmly denied. The family were at the time weak, having been suffering with the fever and ague. The missionary, Mr. B________, and his wife, were the only adult persons in the house. A Sandwich Island man was milking in the barn-yard. The malicious savage evidently chose this opportunity to try his intimidating measures. After much complaining, in which he did most of the talking, he roughly snatched a dress from the hands of Mrs. B________, and flourished his long knife over her head. She seized his arm, and called for her husband, who was in the other room.

Kladakula's attack

As Mr. B______ approached to remonstrate with the savage, he hurled him, with one hand, against the side of the room, and sat himself down in a rocking-chair.

Mr. B______ commenced, in as mild a tone as possible, a remonstrance with him, inquiring why he thus treated them; and appealed to him if he had ever received aught but good at their hands.

But the evil spirit within him was not thus easily tamed. Lifting, in one hand, his flashing steel over his head, he commenced, with the other, to beat Mr. B______, seeming determined to be satisfied only with blood.

Mrs. B______ ran to the yard, and called the friendly Sandwich Islander; but before they returned Kladakula had desisted, and sat down again, as if yet not quite ready for extreme measures.

Some friendly Indians coming in at this moment, Mr. B______ requested them to inquire of Kladakula why he thus treated him, and to remonstrate in his behalf. But they were afraid of him; their superstition making them more afraid of his power as a "medicine man" than of his strength as a chief.

Kladakula again commencing his complaints, Mr. B______ attempted to see if it was possible to pacify him by presenting him a little meal. The savage, with his strong arm, knocked it from his hand, and struck the giver in the breast, so as to nearly render him breathless.

The family were now greatly exhausted, from excitement and the long altercation. Help must come from God, and come soon, or they would faint. They lifted their hearts in prayer, and were reassured that God was near Kladakula rose, and went and sat down in the back room.

Quietly Mrs. B______ prepared her tea; and remembering that it was said, "If thine enemy hunger, feed him," she invited her enemy to eat of her bounty. With the many smiles and blandishments which a savage *can* assume, he sat down and ate.

After supper, seeming to be in a softened mood, Mr. B______ asked Kladakula why he had thus annoyed them.

"O," said he, "because I *bad*, BAD. You good, you do me no hurt. But I *very bad*; I full of *diable*,"—meaning the devil.

It was some time after his departure before the family were fully restored to their wonted peaceful frame of mind; yet their hearts were full of gratitude. They had doubtless been in great danger. Though a great blusterer, Kladakula was very wicked,—a desperate savage,—the terror of the surrounding country God had not permitted him to harm them; and to him they now returned the most heartfelt thanks, and renewedly purposed to trust in him in perils yet to be encountered.

Not long after the above occurrence, Mr. B______ was at work in his workshop, and Kladakula came, saying that he was going among the Klamaths, and they were wicked, and he had no knife to defend himself; he *must* have a knife. This being refused with a decided tone, he seized a carpenter's hatchet, and, springing like a tiger upon a fawn, seized Mr. B_______ in his iron grasp, with one hand, and flourishing, at the same time, the hatchet over his head, yelled, with savage fury, "A knife, a knife! or I'll *kill you!*"

The missionary supposed that his end was near, but a sweet peace took possession of his mind, and a voice seemed to whisper, *"I am with you."* Being determined to show no signs of fear, for he felt none, and being equally decided not to recede from a right position, and thus prepare the way for future aggressions of a similar kind, he looked calmly into the face of the angry savage, and repeated, firmly, "I will *not* give you a knife." The hatchet dropped upon the floor, and Kladakula walked with his *conquerer* into the house!

The missionaries, to preserve their own self-possession, and, if possible, to divert the mind of their angry foe, commenced singing. While thus employed, Kladakula slipped out of the back door, *stole a lasso*, and retired. The lasso was afterward returned by a friendly hand.

The next meeting of the missionary with his tormenter was in his wheat field, when he found him again stealing wheat. On his remonstrating with him, he said, "You never see me more:" and, in mercy to his fellows, and in judgment to him, he never did.

Kladakula went directly to the Berry Ground, and from thence to a village about ten miles above the Dalles. Standing, one day, on the brow of a hill, which rapidly descended into a small stream, a Cayuse Indian crept stealthily toward him, muttering to himself, "You wrong the good Boston; you frighten Indian: you bad, very bad; you live long enough;" and, as he uttered the last word, his rifle cracked, and the deadly bullet pierced the heart of Kladakula.

———•———

### THE BIBLE AND THE HUNTER

The following brief incident contains a great truth, — a truth which God is teaching man, by such facts, every day. It teaches that the Bible is sharper than a two-edged sword.

A large and influential, because energetic and intelligent, class of the inhabitants of Oregon are the hunters. Their life is one of danger and great exposure, but its excitement creates an ardent attachment to it; so that these daring men come to feel as much at home in the forest, on the rugged mountains, and in the frail canoe, as the Indian himself. They are often from the religious and well-educated families of the more eastern portions of the continent; but they seldom retain, in their half-savage life, even good morality. They marry Indian wives, and adopt, to a great extent, the Indian mode of living, with many of their wicked habits.

One of these men, having obtained his accustomed supply of beaver skins, had been down to Vancouver to dispose of them, and, on his return, stopped at the Dalles mission. Having been hospitably entertained, as he was retiring, the missionary put into his hand a copy of God's Word, asking him that he would read it attentively. He took it to his home, far away among the Rocky Mountains. When sitting in his lone camp, he turned over its pages. It spoke to his conscience: it awakened feelings long since stifled. He began to pray, and soon was renewed by the Holy Ghost. He began immediately to publish his new experience; and, by example and precept, labored to win those associated with him to Christ. He became well known afterward as a consistent Christian.

---

## ELIJAH HEDDING

When those devoted missionaries, Jason and Daniel Lee, were on their way to the Willamette Valley, the place of their final location, they formed some acquaintance with many tribes, far in the interior. Some of those tribes, especially the Nez Perces, Cayuses, and Walla-wallas, were desirous to have the missionaries stop with them. This they could not decide to do, but told them, that when they were settled in the Willamette Valley, and had established a school, if they would send their children, they would teach them concerning the white man's way of living, and the white man's God. With this assurance they were pleased, and gave the missionaries several fine horses, and bid them go in peace.

Scarcely had these brethren begun their labor when Pea-pea-mux-mux, the Walla-walla chief, brought his son, to claim of the white teachers the fulfillment of their promise. Of course, his son was cheerfully received, and named Elijah Hedding, after the venerable bishop of that name, who has recently gone to heaven.

Mr. Shephard, whose life is published by the Methodist Sunday-School Union, was his teacher. He labored faithfully, not only to teach Elijah to read, but to lead him to Christ. At a time when many other children were seeking religion, Elijah was convicted of his sinful nature. He said his heart was *bad,—very bad.* After many tears and prayers, he gave good evidence of genuine conversion. He was not what is called "a smart boy;" but, being kind in his disposition and industrious, he improved well.

After Elijah's time had expired for which he was engaged at the mission, he returned to his own tribe, driving a few head of cattle, as the fruit of his industry. Some time subsequent to this, while the brethren whose narrative we are writing were laboring at the Dalles, Elijah came among them, to pursue still further his English education. He had lost the religious enjoyment with which he left the Willamette. The absence of his religious teachers, and the irreligion with which he had been surrounded, had been permitted to overpower his spirit of piety, at least in a measure.

Soon after his arrival at the Dalles, a camp-meeting was held in the vicinity. Elijah attended during the day, and returned to the mission house at night, to perform the little domestic business of the evening. Returning one night with a fellow-Indian, the Spirit of God met him, in great power, by the way. So deep was his conviction, that he returned to the camp ground, craving the prayers of God's people. Earnest and believing supplication was offered in his behalf. The conflict was not long Victory was soon announced in favor of the burdened heart. Elijah arose from his knees, exclaiming, with rapture, "I am rich,—I am rich!" In this happy frame of mind he continued during the acquaintance of the missionaries with him.

Among the female Indian converts was Lahart, a young woman in whom the teachers had taken great interest. Their labor and prayers in her behalf had been rewarded by clear conversion. In her attendance upon the means of grace she was constant. Her efforts of love for unconverted friends, and her consistent dayly walk, won the confidence of her Christian associates. To this pious young woman Elijah was married by one of the missionaries. This was the first marriage solemnity, in a Christian form, that some of the missionaries had seen among the Indians. But, though sincerely loving each other, these persons were not permitted to live happily together. The wife was a *Wascapam,*—the husband a *Walla-walla.* When, soon after their marriage, they removed among *his* tribe, the hatred existing against her people drove her from her husband, and she returned to the Dalles.

The next turn in Elijah's history is a still more sad one. Captain Sutton, of California, had sent a messsage to Elijah's father, the chief, Pea-pea-mux-mux, inviting him to come, with all his good hunters, into the region of his fort, and kill elk and deer, and catch wild horses; and, bringing them into the fort, receive, in return, cattle so highly prized by the Indians. Thus enticed, the chief arrived at Sutter's Fort, with his son Elijah and his principal hunters. He was there reminded that the *branded* horses and mules he might catch belonged to the fort; and, when brought in, he would be paid for catching them: others would be purchased.

Away the hunters started, in high spirits. At times the forests rang with their animated shout; again, they stole silently upon their unsuspecting prey. The sharp crack of the hunter's rifle echoed among the dense woods, and the stately elk and the swift deer lay weltering in their blood.

The party returned to the fort, laden with valuable skins, and driving a number of wild horses; but the *branded* horses and mules had been left behind. The chief had declared that they, having escaped, were no longer Sutton's, and that he should not have them. This the people of the fort learned at a moment when Elijah was with them, but his father and most of his people were in their camp. In an angry tone, they demanded of Elijah the instant surrender of the animals.

"I," replied the undaunted Christian, "have spoken in favor of their return; but *my father is the chief*."

This surely was a sufficient answer; but the angry attitude of his enemies convinced Elijah that his life was in danger. He knew, too, the wickedness of the savage white men. He calmly remarked, "If I am to die, give me time to pray;" and, while assuming an attitude of devotion, he was shot dead!

All that was known of Elijah, from the time of the camp-meeting, was favorable to his consistent piety. His resort to prayer in his hour of trial, his firm integrity in opposition to his father's dishonesty, give evidence that his heart was still right before God. How pleasing to think that, through missionary labor, there was hope in his death!

On learning his son's fate, Pea-pea-mux-mux fled precipitately with his company; leaving all his cattle—the avails of his enterprise—to his enemies.

————•————

### THE POWER OF CONSCIENCE

"Indians will steal," said a distinguished statesman, who had been the government's Indian agent in the north-west territory. Though, through the power of the gospel, there have been many pleasing exceptions to this remark, yet it expresses a general characteristic of the red man. How are we to expect it to be otherwise? They have but lately heard of the Bible. The white men, who are their acknowledged superiors, and who have known the commandment, "Thou shalt not steal," have practiced the most cruel thefts upon the poor Indian himself. Too many of them have known only the unprincipled trader, or the reckless pioneer emigrant, who neither "deal justly" nor "walk uprightly."

Much of the perplexity of the missionaries' labor arose from the thieving propensity of those whom they would win to Christ. The following incident will illustrate this remark.

There was a man living near the mission station, whom his companions called Waketla. He was a Wisham, but lived among the Wascapams. He was intelligent and active. His skill as a "canoe-man" made him quite useful. In various other ways he had rendered service to the missionaries; and they, in return, had imparted to him important instruction in religion and the practices of civilized life. He was attentive, and at times seemed benefited by what he learned.

One day he was employed chopping wood at the mission door. He stepped in frequently to the back room for water, and, at one time, his eye rested upon a silver spoon, which had been, contrary to the practice and intention of its owner, left in a tempting place. Waketla looked this way and that, to see if *man* saw him; but forgot to look *up*, remembering that *God's* eyes see everything. His wicked heart said, "They will not miss it; white men are rich, — Indian poor." But conscience said, "It is not yours. It is wrong to steal." But conscience was *talked down*, and the spoon carried to his lodge.

One sin seldom stands alone. Crime makes way for crime. The spoon was seen by one of his fellow-Indians, to whom he protested that he had received it from the hand of the missionary's wife. Not believing his story, his companion hasted away to the station, and inquired, "You lose spoon, — a *dollar spoon?*" meaning silver spoon. "Indian got one, — Waketla. He say white woman give him. No, no," shaking his head; "no believe: me know Waketla steal him."

Soon after Waketla came in, when something like the following conversation took place: —

"Waketla!" said the housekeeper.

"Umph!" was the reply.

"I have treated you kindly, — taught you many things Indians don't know, so that you think you are almost 'a Boston.' You have heard the preaching, and you have attended to the prayer-meetings. You say that you pray, and mean to be good." During this conversation, the culprit had straightened up, and stood listening, as if in anticipation of some important relevation. "But, Waketla," added his reprover, solemnly, lowering her voice, "you steal!" putting the truth home, as Nathan did to David.

Waketla's head fell upon his bosom, and he slunk back into a chair, guilt speaking in every feature, and in every act.

"Now," continued his teacher, "God saw you, and is displeased. He will not hear when you pray, unless you repent. You never can be happy until you return the spoon, ask God to forgive you, and try to do so no more. Your act was mean and wicked. You wronged your best friends. Waketla must now be 'brave to do right,' and faint when wrong tempts him.' "

The next morning, early, Waketla came with the spoon, his countenance showing a self-approving conscience. He handed it to its owner, saying, "Your talk was good yesterday. Ah, Indian no feel right! No pray, — no feel brave when I see white teacher. I look up in the night through the trees, see the stars shine, and think they God's eyes looking at Waketla. Me no have peace here," striking upon his breast. "Now I feel good, —no steal more."

Waketla's bitter experience was not soon forgotten, we trust. The gospel had given him a conscience which would not let him sin unreproved. It taught him the only way to relieve a troubled breast, —"To confess and forsake his sin."

**The stolen spoon**

## PEACEFUL DYING

The records of the triumphant departure from earth to heaven of the good in Christian lands find a place in the pages of our religious papers. These records stimulate the pious zeal of God's people. Shall not the servants of Christ, saved by the cross from heathen darkness, be permitted to let their light shine, even amid the light of a Christian land?

Simeon was an old man, among the Indians of Oregon, when he was brought to God: but so much meekness and ripeness of experience did he soon show, that they suggested the Christian name, Simeon. He was very constant in his visits to his closet; he evidently met God there. He delighted in the circle for social prayer. In his family he was faithful, endeavoring to lead his household to God. His name was without reproach, so blameless was his life before all men.

After he was taken sick, the missionaries visited him, with medicine for the body; endeavoring also to strengthen his faith for his last conflict, which was evidently near. But Simeon's house was in order, and he was ready to die. His religious teachers were not permitted to be with him in his last moments. His son, who witnessed his triumph over death, said to the missionary, "O, he no die like other Indians! He happy, happy! He say angels come to take him away, —they be in his lodge, —they be all around!"

"Such is the Christian's parting hour;
*So peacefully he sinks to rest.*"

Chocalalite was a chief of the Wascapams. He was brave, but modest and dignified. He discharged his duties to his people faithfully. He married a beautiful woman of the Walla-wallas. There was not a more agreeable couple, nor a more interesting family of children than was theirs, among all the Indians of the vicinity. The parents would come often, and make a call upon the mission family, perhaps to spend an evening. To secure a welcome, they would pleasantly remark, as they entered, that they had not come to beg. Chocalalite was one of the few Indians who was too high-minded to indulge in this almost universal practice of his race. Their company, on these occasions, was really pleasing. They conversed readily concerning the great topics of practical religion, for they had given evidence of sound conversion. Their children, when they accompanied their parents, would prattle away, either in their mother's native language, the Walla-walla, or their father's, the Wascapam. The light of religion, and consequent civilization, had brought joy into this family. They were deeply conscious of their obligation to it, and loved its solemn assemblies. They were like a fruitful tree which had sprung up beside a gushing spring, in the midst of a barren desert. But consumption marked Chocalalite for its victim. He grew paler dayly, and his once erect and manly frame began to bow beneath its influence. He could no longer join in the fishing excursion, nor follow the panting deer. With a feeble step he would go to the place of prayer, while his heart was becoming more and more fitted for the inheritance of the just.

He spoke of his approaching death with great composure, and gave directions concerning his funeral, being particular to direct that the whole ceremony should be after the Christian practice. His affectionate wife sorrowed with no affected grief while she anticipated his death. He gradually failed, day by day, until, almost imperceptibly, his earthly pilgrimage ceased. Peacefully, and with unshaken confidence in a glorious immortality, he fell asleep in Jesus.

Tirash was a young man. His aged father had been, for many years, a letter-carrier to the Hudson's Bay Company, — an office of great responsibility. Tirash had succeeded his father in this business, much to the old man's joy, and the satisfaction of the company. He was an only son, and the pride of his intelligent though unconverted father. To him he committed the care of his property, consisting principally of horses; and the son never betrayed the trust thus committed to him.

He had professed faith in Christ, and God was about to put to the test of a dying hour the genuineness of that faith. The dysentery had proved a terrible disease to the poor Indians, very many of them having died suddenly under its power. With this Tirash was taken sick. His father called in the aid of Elymas, the medicine man; but he grew sicker, and the afflicted parent sought the aid of the missionaries. When he consented to dismiss Elymas, they undertook to administer medicine to the sinking young man; but it was too late, — death had marked him for his own!

Looking calmly and with a pleasant smile upon his weeping father, he said, "Father, do not weep for me. I am going to heaven. Yes, I am going to be with Christ!" Thus triumphantly he passed away.

His aged parent refused to be comforted. "I feel," he exclaimed, "that I am cut through. There is nothing left of me: I am as dead."

The above examples will be sufficient to convince our young readers that religion in the heart of a heathen, as well as among the inhabitants of Christian lands, gives victory over death and the grave.

----•----

### THE RETURN HOME

When the missionaries first began their labors in Oregon, it was very difficult to obtain the means of support without devoting much time to the clearing of lands, and becoming, to a considerable extent, farmers. This would take too much of the attention of those who had the language of the country to learn, to preach to the Indians, and to instruct them constantly in religious truths. This made it necessary to have farmers and mechanics attached to the mission, — men of God, who, while they provided means of support to the whole mission company, could do much good by teaching the Indians to cultivate the lands, and to work at useful trades. They could, at the same time, be of great service in the religious exercises of the mission. But, as the country became more settled, and the missions fully established, such laborers were not so much needed as ordained ministers of the gospel. Therefore, our friends, whose history in Oregon we have slightly sketched, after an absence of nearly nine years, prepared to return home.

It was not strange that scenes which had been associated with suffering, labor, dangers, and religious enjoyments, should have become very dear to them. The very mountains, covered with snow, upon which they had so often gazed; the Columbia, sweeping over its rocky bed; the forests, vocal with the song of birds; the old mission premises, in their very rudeness, especially the humble chapel, where the voice of prayer and praise had so often heard; *all* seemed lovely.

But the Indians, though at times savage, and always betraying the effects of their long degradation by sin; were loved still: especially did the few who had been the fruits of Christian labor, — who had shown themselves faithful, — who were loved for the solicitude even which they had occasioned, — call forth the warmest emotions at parting. Some accompanied them awhile in their journey toward the sea, and then parted, "sorrowing most of all that they should see their faces no more."

A part of their journey to the vessel was performed by aid of an ox-team, and was necessarily slow and tedious. At night they were slightly sheltered from the cool air, and their wearied limbs reposed on no downy beds; but they were used to these primitive customs, and were cheerful and happy.

The parting with their co-laborers in the Willamette Valley, some of whom had been immediate sharers of their sacrifices, was sad, yet joyful. Sad, because they might never meet again on earth; joyful, since they recollected the goodness of God, of which they had been the mutual sharers, and because they expected to meet in heaven.

They embarked at Vancouver, on board the brig *Eveline*, May 7, 1848; and, with a fair wind and a skillful pilot, safely passed the dreaded bar at the mouth of the Columbia. But the pilot was not so fortunate in returning. The wind suddenly failing, his barge was drawn from the channel by a strong current, and dashed to pieces upon the rocks. All the crew, by a kind Providence, were saved.

After a pleasant sail of eighteen days from the Columbia, they reached Honolulu, one of the Sandwich Islands, without any occurrence of marked interest. There they were obliged to wait three and a half months for an opportunity to get a passage to the States. Their stay was made as pleasant as the circumstances allowed, by the Christian kindness of the missionaries of the American Board.

The climate of the island, though pleasant, not being so invigorating as the colder air of the northern States, the missionaries suffered from a feeling of lassitude and feebleness.

On the 7th of September they gladly stepped on board the ship *South America*, bound for Providence, R.I. She was a whale ship, laden with five thousand five hundred barrels of oil; taken mostly from whales in the Japan seas. The officers of the ship were kind, and the accommodations good. Thus had God provided for his servants, after their long separation from home, a comfortable means of return.

In passing around Cape Horn, their attention was attracted by the Cape pigeon, the spotted eaglets, and the petrels, gliding gracefully just above the crested wave, seeming to have their home on the deep.

After passing the Cape, our voyagers experienced a series of contrary winds, and severe gales; while the sea tossed their noble ship upon its towering billows, as if it had been a bubble of its own foam. One night, when they were all quietly slumbering in their state-rooms, the vessel "shipped a sea," that is, she plunged into the bosom of a wave, instead of rising on its swelling top, and the waters swept over her deck, seeming, for a moment, to have buried her in its depths forever. Her tall masts quivered, and her whole frame trembled under the concussion. Instantly, all on board started to their feet. Even the experienced sailor was alarmed. But kindly did God care for them: the ship rose bravely to her place upon the surface of the sea, and glided forward on her course unharmed.

On the 30th of November, Pernambuco, South America, **was seen** in the distance; appearing like a city rising out of the ocean. Here **they obtained** fresh provisions, which were peculiarly pleasing to the *eye*, as well as **refreshing** to the taste, wearied as they were with the monotony of the sea life and diet.

Without further incident of note, they reached their destined port.

We will not intrude upon the sacred moment of meeting with parents and friends, whom God had spared to meet them on their return. Deeply interesting was the occasion; but of more thrilling interest will that moment be when the good of all lands shall come up before God, having been redeemed by the blood of Christ, to sit *together* with him forever!

**THE END**

# Index

# COLOPHON

*The Zacharia Atwell Mudge* SKETCHES OF MISSION LIFE AMONG THE INDIANS OF OREGON, *was printed in the workshop of Glen Adams, which is located in the sleepy country village of Fairfield, southern Spokane County, Washington State. The text was set in type by Dale La Tendresse using a 7300 Editwriter computer photosetter. The setting is in eleven point Baskerville roman with page numbers in twelve point Baskerville Bold, and running heads in nine point Baskerville roman. Camera-darkroom work was by Evelyn Foote Clausen. The film was stripped, opaqued and plates made by Robert La Tendresse, who also printed the sheets using a 770CD Hamada offset press. The sheets were folded by Sydney Stevens Jr. using an air-operated Baum folding machine. General book design was by Glen Adams who also did the color imprinting using a 14x22 open platen press, a Chandler & Price, vintage 1928. This platen press is an old friend, as Glen has owned it for more than twenty years. Assembly of the books was by Kristy Frisbie Mayfield. Indexing was by Dale La Tendresse. The paper stock is sixty pound Simpson Opaque in a wove finish. Binding is by Willem Bosch of Oakesdale, Washington. This was a fun project. We had no special difficulty with the work.*

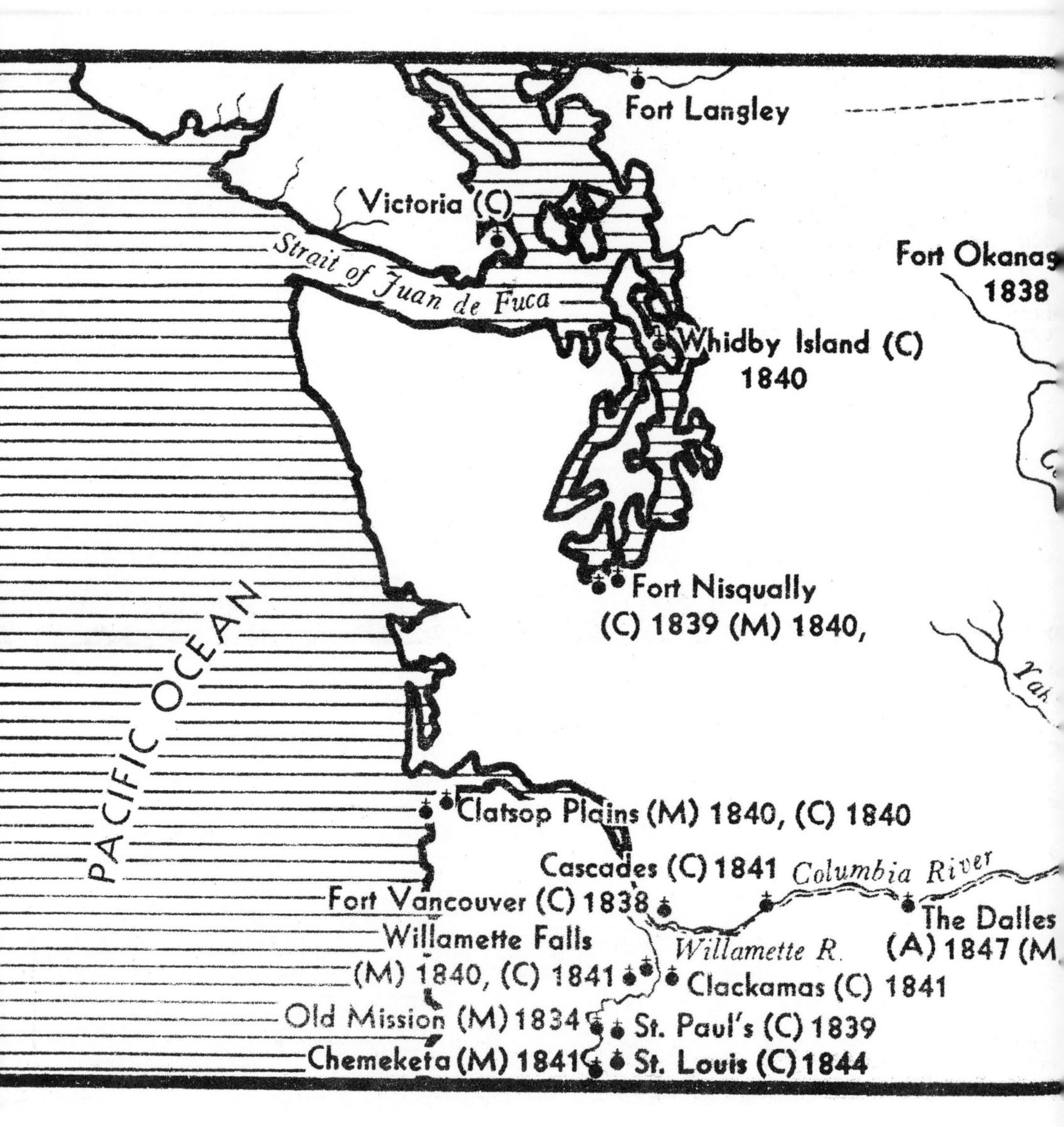

Fort Langley
Victoria (C)
Fort Okanag
1838
Strait of Juan de Fuca
Whidby Island (C)
1840
PACIFIC OCEAN
Fort Nisqually
(C) 1839 (M) 1840,
Yak
Clatsop Plains (M) 1840, (C) 1840
Cascades (C) 1841
Columbia River
Fort Vancouver (C) 1838
The Dalles
Willamette Falls
Willamette R.
(A) 1847 (M
(M) 1840, (C) 1841
Clackamas (C) 1841
Old Mission (M) 1834
St. Paul's (C) 1839
Chemeketa (M) 1841
St. Louis (C) 1844